The End of Freedom

How our Monetary System Enslaves Us

by John Thore Stub Sneisen of The Economic Truth

Published in Canada by:

Courunne Publishing

© Copyright 2015 – John Thore Stub Sneisen

1st Edition

ISBN-13: 978-0-9948637-0-6

ALL RIGHTS RESERVED. No part of this publication may be reproduced or transmitted in any form whatsoever, electronic, or mechanical, including photocopying, recording, or by any informational storage or retrieval system without express written, dated and signed permission from the author.

Table of Contents

Foreword by G. Edward Griffin 7

Dedication 11

Introduction 13
    A Brief History of Fiat Currency 13
    Ask Yourself These Questions 18
Chapter 1: Inflation: The Destruction of Wealth 21

    The History of Currency Devaluation:
    Coinage 21

    Taking Without Asking: A Government Point
    of View 29

    The Discovery of Paper Currency and The
    Delusion of Value 32

    The Graveyard of Money 34

    Fiat Currencies Currently on Death Row 83

Chapter 2: Papered Over: The Worthless History of
Fiat Paper Currencies 1000 Year Reign 93

China's First Paper Currencies 94
Unlimited National Debt in Austria 100
The Ottoman Empire 105
The Mississippi Bubble and The French Revolution 107
Weimar Republic (Germany) 118
Bulgarian Leva Devaluation.......................... 125
Yugoslavia... 126
Argentina... 135
Zimbabwe.. 152
The 2008 Crisis 160
The Arab Spring 169
Current Economic Turmoil and War In Ukraine 179
Current Venezuela Inflation Caused By Low Oil Price.. 190
Greece's Big Government and The Destruction of an Economy and Its People 197

Chapter 3: Government Slaves: Austerity 208

Chapter 4: Bail In: The Real Risk of Having Money in Your Bank Account 215

Chapter 5: The Rise of The Corporate Fascism: Collusion and The Rise of Monopolies.................. 221

    The Military Industrial Complex................ 223

    Big Agra/Food Corporations...................... 226

    Big Pharma.. 233

    Big Oil... 235

    Prison Industrial Complex(USA)............... 240

Chapter 6: Interest Rate Apartheid: The New Black is Bad Credit 243

Chapter 7: International Money Fraud................... 246

    IMF (International Monetary Fund) or International Money Fraud.......................... 246

    IMF and Austerity Measures: The SDR...... 247

    The BIS - The Central Bank of The World 263

Chapter 8: The Current Destruction of Currencies: A Global Problem 268

Chapter 9: The Death of The Middle Class: The Rise of Rich and Poor 308

Conclusion 315
    The Problem With Fiat Currency and
    Fractional Reserve Banking 315
    Bail Out of Bankrupt Organizations............ 324
    Famous Quotes about Central Banking and
    Fiat Currency: A Warning From History 329

Refrences 338

Suggested Reading 340

Foreword

There are several things about books that make them my absolute top choice for preserving and conveying important information. Not only are they portable and convenient to access regardless of location, but they are about as tamper-proof as it gets in terms of preventing information from being corrupted by guardians of political correctness. It is true that books can be burned or forged, but that is far more difficult than editing digital files in a master computer.

This is the thought that crossed my mind as I contemplated the substance of the book you are about to read, and it made me smile to think that what is written here has the potential to last for hundreds of years.

Speaking of such long historical cycles may seem a bit useless in the rapidly changing world of today, and some people may say that doing so is just academic rhetoric. Who cares about a hundred years from now when the outcome of the next election may change the world!

That argument has the sound of truth, but it is only half true. Let us restate it with the other half included:

"The outcome of the next election may change the world, but the next election will be determined by ideas that were planted in society a hundred years ago."

There is no better illustration of this than looking at what has happened to the United States. The US Constitution was an amazing document for many reasons. Perhaps its most significant accomplishment is that it is the first successful political charter that established a state in which the sovereign power was declared to be the people instead of the monarch.

A careful reading of the Constitution reveals that, although it speaks of creating a government, actually, it created a protectorate. The intent was not to govern the people but to protect them. Specifically, it was to protect the lives, liberty, and property of its citizens. In other words, the Constitution was the word's first political charter that embodied the ideology of individualism.

Because it was a beta model, it should not be surprising that it was not perfect. The Founders were navigating unchartered waters, and it was necessary to compromise on many issues in order to secure ratification from all the colonies. There were some issues that were deliberately left vague knowing that future clarification would be required, and some issues were removed from the document altogether. In other words, as brilliant as the Constitution was in concept, it was compromised at the very beginning as a necessity for its birth. With clauses such as "for the general welfare" the seeds of collectivism were implanted in the original soil and began to sprout immediately.

It is shocking to read some of the early accounts of American history and realize that many of the insults to the liberty of Americans that have surfaced in modern times have roots that run all the way back to the Constitutional Convention.

This fact is not justification to condemn the Constitution or the men who created it. They did the best that was humanly possible under the circumstances. Considering the roadblocks in their way, it is truly amazing that this beta model was as good as it was. For a hundred years, it enabled the greatest burst of productivity, creativity, and liberty the world had ever seen. It took a hundred years for the seeds and weeds of collectivism to finally choke out the flowers of enterprise and liberty.

Now it's our turn to continue the revolution of ideas. It's our turn to build on the successes and learn from the failures of the beta model and create an improved model for the next generation. (1) To create a safe path between past and future, we must have the long view of history. We must look further ahead than the next election. We must understand that, through books like the one you are about to read, seeds are being planted today that have the potential to become the political forests of tomorrow. The outcome of the "next election" for our great grandchildren is being determined as we speak.

G. Edward Griffin
2015 September 29

(1) That is one of the goals of Freedom Force International, an organization that John and I wholeheartedly recommend and support.
http://wp.freedomforceinternational.org

Dedication

This book is dedicated to my beautiful and loving wife Quinn who always supports my work, and to my parents who always have believed in me to do well in this world. It is also dedicated to all of you who are reading this information for the first time and become awakened and take action to pass this information to friends and family and other people they care about. I also want to dedicate this book to all the victims of the current monetary system and say to all of you there is still hope!!!

I want to thank all of my 100's mentors and teachers through the last 8 years of research into the world of money, economics and geopolitics.

Finance and geopolitics. I want to bring out a special thanks to G. Edward Griffin and the Leadership Council of Freedom Force International who has been one of my motivating forces to take action. I also want to thank all of my great friends from around the world who has brought me great stories and insights into their lives.

I also want to thank my friend Osamede who without his help this book would still be just thoughts.

I also want to thank Josh from World Alternative Media for helping me spreading the word.

I lastly want to thank my sister Anne for all the help!

Introduction

A brief history of Fiat Currency

Why do I believe the current Fiat Currency and Fractional Reserve banking system is a failure and a breach of your human rights? Why choose to remain enslaved in debt slavery!

The invention of paper money has been dated to China in 1000 AD.

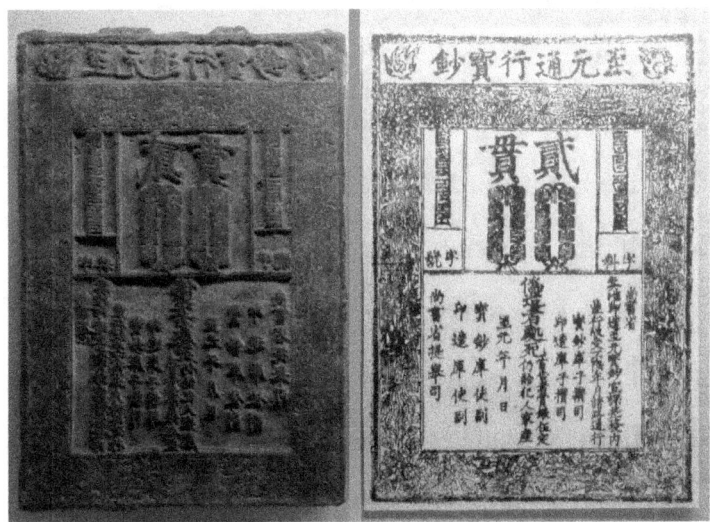

Yuan dynasty banknotes are the earliest known fiat money.

Fiat money is currency which derives its value from government regulation or law. The term is derived from the Latin word *fiat* ("let it be done", "it shall be"). It differs from both commodity as well as representative money. Commodity money is based on a good, often a precious metal such as gold or silver, which has uses other than as a medium of exchange, while representative money is a claim on the commodity rather than the actual good. Fiat currency is forced on citizens. They have to accept it or risk imprisonment if they choose not to want to use it as money. There is no choice and the only thing that backs a fiat currency is the trust of the people using it.

The first use of fiat money was recorded in China around 1000 AD. Since then, it has been used continuously by various countries concurrently with commodity currencies.

I have worked for a long time and gathered evidence that our current monetary systems, which have failed over 600 times throughout history, have always destroyed those people who are not in control of it, but use it. There are several examples where banks, governments and other institutions take away the rights of the people after blowing up the system themselves.

A collapse of monetary system will be inevitable if we continue to use the Fiat Currency and Fractional Reserve Banking Systems. Many countries choose a Zero Reserve Policy (which means the bank decides its own deposit to loan ratio) as an option from Fractional Reserve Banking. All of these systems are a breach of our fundamental human and individual rights.

Ask yourself this

Should we give any organization or government the power to destroy the wealth we have built for ourselves? Wealth that we have accumulated for when we grow older and want to relax more and work less? Is it okay for governments to enforce their created-out-of-thin-air currency upon us to use for what we need if we value gold, silver, beads, bartering, oil, wheat, or even avocados as mediums of exchange?

Ask yourself these questions!

Is it okay to let them take your wealth and freeze it overnight so you cannot access it and then inform you the next day that you now have 75% less wealth?

Is it okay for bankers to get paid dividends on the money created in a nation?

Is it okay to give a loan in a global currency to a country like Ukraine to support them to buy arms to fight the side we don't like?

Is it okay for bankers to crash an economy by making bad decisions and then getting the assets back for nothing?

Is it okay for banks to take all or most of your money if they fail? Well, if you knew how they operated you would not want to put your money in one of them.

Is it okay to have massive inequality caused by printing of currency and giving it to the rich to become richer by pumping up asset prices?

Is it okay to print so much money that no one can buy anything with their salary while the people who get the money buy everything and consolidate power?

Is it okay to charge interest (money that does not exist) when someone borrows money and then they are forced to work and charged income tax to pay the government's interest charges?

Is it okay to remove valuable metals from people's coins to print more money and not let them know they are losing their purchasing power?

Let's take a look at some violations that happen when FIAT Currency and/or Fractional Reserve Banking is put in place in economies around the world!

Chapter One
Inflation: The Destruction of Your Wealth

The History of Currency Devaluation: Coinage

From Wikipedia[1]

Debasement is the practice of lowering the value of currency. It is used particularly in connection with commodity money such as gold or silver coins. A coin is said to be debased if the quantity of gold, silver, copper or nickel is reduced.

The history of currency debasement of coins starts all the way back from the Greek Empire.

---

[1] Definition from Wikipedia

Examples

The Roman Empire

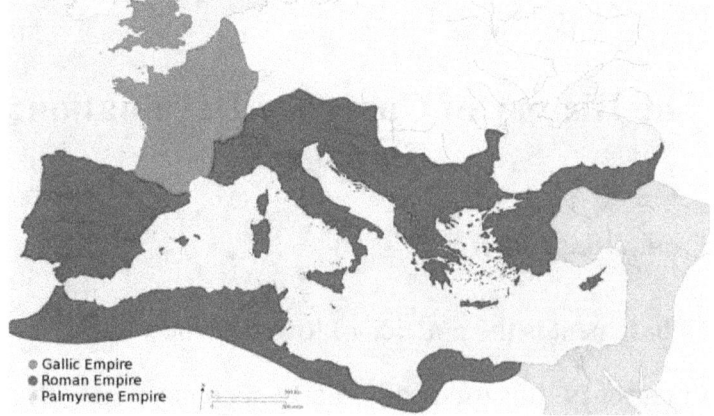

The most notorious coin debaser and over 200+ years they devalued their Denariuses to only 2% silver from 100% around year 190. For example, the value of the denarius in Roman currency gradually decreased over time as the Roman government altered both the size and the silver content of the coin. Originally, the silver used was nearly pure, weighing about 4.5 grams. From time to time, this was reduced. During the Julio-Claudian dynasty, the Denarius contained approximately 4 grams of silver, which was then was reduced to 3.8 grams under Nero. The Denarius continued to shrink in size and purity, until by the second half of the third century it was only about 2% silver, and was replaced by the Argenteus.

The Vijayanagara Empire of India

Because of its coffers of huge wealth, the Vijayanagara Empire issued large quantities of gold coins. Harihara-I and Bukka (the founders of the famous Vijayanagara Empire in South India) minted gold coins using debased gold. Gold Fanams (a type of coin) and their fractions were minted by them for medium-end transactions.

These empires debased their currencies and subsequently collapsed their societies. Roman coinage from year 211AD and earlier maintained their purchasing power because the coins were made from 90% of gold and silver. Meanwhile in today's paper currency systems the paper holds no real value standing alone, and only continue to devalue in today's markets when an increased amount is placed into circulation.

The longest lasting empire in history - the Ottoman Empire: Debasement lowers the intrinsic value of the coinage and so more coins can be made with the same quantity of precious metal. Debasement was by itself not a source of inflation, but it could have been so if the King spent the extra financing capacity too quickly and unproductively. The cause of inflation in medieval times is found in the type of expenditure that Kings did rather than the ability to debase. Wars, huge castles, and other extravagant and unproductive expenses strained the resources of the economy. If the debased currency had been used methodically to fund projects that promoted economic growth, high inflation would not have occurred. If done too frequently, debasement could lead to a new coin being adopted as standard currency, just as when the Ottoman Akçe was replaced by the Kuruş (1 kurus = 120 akçe), with the para (1/40 kurus) as a subunit. The

Kurus later became a subdivision of the lira. This leads us to the next crime of Fiat Currencies, Devaluation and Inflation, as the Akce was replaced 1 to 120 by a new currency but the value of the new currency was basically the same.

Canada debased their currency

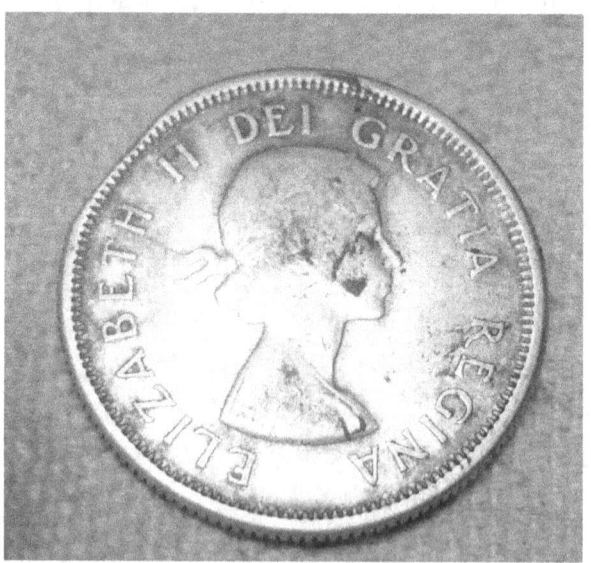

By removing silver from their coinage in 1968. The 10¢ and higher denominations were debased, their silver alloy replaced by nickel. In 2000, all coins below $1 were changed to steel with copper or nickel plating; in 2012, this was extended to the $1 and $2 coins as well. The 50¢ piece is regularly minted, but not in large quantities; it is very rare to come across this coin in circulation, although an unsuccessful attempt was made by the Mint to promote the use of the coin when a special edition was released in 2002 marking the 50th anniversary of Elizabeth II ascending the throne.

Stealing of money from citizens is history's number one reason for currency debasement!

One reason a government will debase its currency is financial gain for the sovereign at the expense of citizens. By reducing the silver or gold content of a coin, a government can make more coins out of a given amount of specie. Inflation follows, allowing the sovereign to pay off or repudiate government bonds with currency that's worth is less, but that has the same face value. However, the purchasing power of the citizens' currency has been reduced. Another reason is to end a deflationary spiral, meaning that the economy contracts and the government or banks wants to keep their power and pay off their debt with newly inflated currency that has less value, but the money borrowed stays the same.

Deflation makes the debt borrowed more expensive and almost impossible to pay back as the money supply decreases.

When it reaches a point where many people do this, then you know you have printed far too much currency of the metal backing it. Debasement in modern days is caused more by paper currency overflow and undermining the value of the metal in the coinage. That is why most countries that used to have gold and silver coinage have ever since left precious metal in their coinage in order to print more money and steal more of your wealth! Many countries perform debasement in order to go to war. Modern day debasement is created more through reckless money printing by bankers and governments.

Taking Without Asking: A Government's Point of View

What **mainstream media**, government and **schools would te**ach **about** currency **debasement: it is to prevent counterfeiting of money and people melting down the money.**

Debasement was also the result of the value of the precious metal content rising above the face value of coins. As the market price of precious metal rose, the intrinsic value of coins would eventually rise above the face value and so a profit could be made from using coins as bullion rather than as monetary instrument. This gave an incentive to money changers and mint masters to practice illegal debasement via clipping (shaving metal from the coin's circumference) and sweating (shaking the coins in a bag and collecting the dust worn off). Coins would also be melted down and exported. To anticipate these illegal debasements and preserve the quality and quantity of coins, the king would either debase or cry up the coinage (i.e. raise the face value of coins). Thus, debasement had its legitimate purposes and was welcomed by the population if done to preserve the stability of the coinage by manipulating the true value of it.

«Debasement kills the value of your saved up wealth and is therefore a crime of an empire, country or state as it steals from you and makes you poor for no other reason but to spend more money without your consent» - John Sneisen

The Discovery of Paper Currency and the Delusion of Value

A point of view from explorer Marco Polo:
"All these pieces of paper are, issued with as much solemnity and authority as if they were of pure gold or silver and indeed everybody takes them readily, for wheresoever a person may go throughout the Great Kaan's dominions

he shall find these pieces of paper current, and shall be able to transact all sales and purchases of goods by means of them just as well as if they were coins of pure gold." —Marco Polo, The Travels of Marco Polo[2]

---

[2] Quote taken from Marco Polo's book the Travels of Marco Polo

Let's take a look at different destructions of currencies around the world:

Song Dynasty of China introduced the practice of printing paper money in order to create fiat currency. During the Mongol Yuan Dynasty, the government spent a great deal of money fighting costly wars, and reacted by printing more currency, leading to inflation. The problem of inflation became so severe that the people stopped using paper money, which they saw as "worthless paper." Fearing the inflation that plagued the Yuan dynasty, the Ming Dynasty initially rejected the use of paper money, using only copper coins. The dynasty did not issue paper currency until 1375.

The Graveyard of Money
A historical look at Fiat Paper Currencies

The historical period for which they lasted

(Remember: FIAT currencies only get their value by

force from governments, private institutions and your belief that it is a valid medium of exchange):

Currency Name (Currency Code)	Inception	Demonetized	Duration (Years)	Destroyed by Hyperinflation
DDR Kuponmark (DDK)	1948	1948	1 mo.	Yes
Yugoslav 1994 Dinar (YUG)	1994	1994	1 mo.	Yes
Hungarian Bilpengoe (HUB)	1946	1946	1.5 mos.	Yes
German Gold Mark (DEG)	1923	1923	2 mos.	Yes
Hungarian Adopengoe (HUA)	1946	1946	2 mos.	Yes
Netherlands Rijksdaalder (NLX)	1904	1904	2.5 mos.	
Slovenia Laibach Lira (SIL)	1944	1944	2.5 mos.	
Hungarian Milpengoe (HUM)	1946	1946	3 mos.	Yes

North Korean Won (KPO)	1959	1959	3 mos.	Yes
Kazakhstan Ruble (KZR)	1993	1993	3 mos.	Yes
Yugoslav October Dinar (YUO)	1993	1993	3 mos.	Yes
Krajina (Serbian Republic) October Dinar (HRKO)	1993	1994	3 mos.	Yes
Polish Zloty Lublin (PLL)	1944	1945	4 mos.	
Serbian Republic October Dinar (BASO)	1993	1994	4 mos.	
Hungarian Red Army Pengoe (HUR)	1945	1945	6 mos.	Yes
Rupiah Kepulauan Riau (IDRR)	1963	1964	8.5 mos.	
Uzbekistan Coupon Sum (UZC)	1993	1994	8.5 mos.	Yes
Japan Base Metal Kammon (JPK)	1904	1905	9 mos.	Yes
Japan Silver Momme (JPM)	1904	1905	9 mos.	Yes
Japan Gold Oban (JPO)	1904	1905	9 mos.	Yes

Lithuania Talonas (LTT)	1992	1993	9 mos.	Yes
Ukraine Karbovanetz (UAK)	1992	1993	11 mos.	Yes
Transnistrian Ruble (PDR)	1994	1994	11 mos.	Yes
French Franc (Assignats) (FRA)	1795	1796	1	Yes
French Franc (Mandats Territorial) (FRM)	1796	1797	1	Yes
Confederate States Reformed Dollar (CSAR)	1864	1865	1	Yes
German New Guinea Mark (PGM)	1914	1915	1	
German Southwest Africa Mark (NAP)	1914	1915	1	
Transcaucasian Ruble (ZKRR)	1917	1918	1	
Austrian Krone (ATK)	1918	1919	1	
North Russian Ruble (RUNR)	1919	1920	1	
East Africa Florin (XEAF)	1920	1922	1	
Russian Ruble	1922	1922	1	Yes

of 1922 (RUFR)				
Soviet Ruble of 1923 (SUB)	1923	1924	1	Yes
Austrian Allied Military Schillings (ATM)	1944	1945	1	
Czechoslovak Red Army Korunu (CSR)	1944	1945	1	
Romanian Red Army Leu (ROR)	1944	1945	1	Yes
Azerbaijan Toman (IRZT)	1945	1946	1	
Sinkiang Gold Yuan (CNSG)	1948	1949	1	
Chinese Gold Chin Yuan (CNG)	1948	1949	1	Yes
Ghana Old Cedi (GHO)	1965	1967	1	
Brazil Cruzado Novo (BRN)	1989	1990	1	Yes
Slovenia Tolar Bons (SIB)	1991	1992	1	
Moldovan Ruble Kupon (MDR)	1991	1992	1	Yes
Moldovan Leu Cupon (MDC)	1992	1993	1	
Albanian Lek Valute (ALV)	1992	1993	1	

Serbian Republic Reformed Dinar (BASR)	1992	1993	1	Yes
Krajina (Serbian Republic) Reformed Dinar (HRKR)	1992	1993	1	Yes
Latvia Ruble (LVR)	1992	1993	1	Yes
Macedonian Denar (MKN)	1992	1993	1	Yes
Yugoslav Reformed Dinar (YUR)	1992	1993	1	Yes
Brazil Cruzeiro Real (BRR)	1993	1994	1	Yes
Maryland Red Shillings (CMDR)	1781	1783	2	
New Jersey New Shilling (CNJN)	1781	1783	2	
Vermont State Shilling (CVTS)	1781	1783	2	
Haiti New Paper Gourde (HTN)	1870	1872	2	Yes
Peru Inca (PER)	1880	1882	2	
Germany Darlenskasse Ost Ruble (DEOR)	1916	1918	2	
Armenian Ruble (AMR)	1918	1920	2	

Azerbaijan Republic Ruble (AZR)	1918	1920	2
Khiva Tenga (KHVT)	1918	1920	2
Soviet Armenian Ruble (AMSR)	1920	1922	2
Soviet Azerbaijan Ruble (AZSR)	1920	1922	2
Far Eastern Republic Ruble (DBRR)	1920	1922	2
Soviet Transcaucasian Ruble (ZKSR)	1922	1924	2
Spanish Nationalist Peseta (ESPN)	1936	1939	2
Reichs Karbowanez (UAC)	1942	1944	2
US "Hawaiian" Dollar (USDH)	1942	1944	2
Italy American Military Lira (ITA)	1943	1945	2
Italy British Military Lira (ITB)	1943	1945	2
Italy "Badaglio" Lira (ITLB)	1943	1945	2
Italy	1943	1945	2

"Mussolini" Lira (ITLM)				
Korean Military Won (KROM)	1945	1947	2	
French Franc Nouveau (FRF)	1960	1962	2	
Biafran Pound (BIAP)	1968	1970	2	
Oman Rial Saidi (OMS)	1970	1972	2	
Argentina Peso Argentino (ARP)	1983	1985	2	Yes
Yugoslav Convertible Dinar (YUN)	1990	1992	2	Yes
Belarus Ruble (BYL)	1992	1994	2	
Bosnia Dinar (BAD)	1992	1994	2	Yes
Georgia Kupon Larit (GEK)	1993	1995	2	Yes
Krajina (Serbian Republic) 1994 Dinar (HRKG)	1994	1996	2	Yes
Maryland Black Shillings (CMDB)	1780	1783	3	
Confederate States Dollar (CSAD)	1861	1864	3	
Mexico "Inconvertible"	1913	1916	3	

Paper Peso (MXI)				
Georgian Ruble (GER)	1918	1921	3	
Danzig Mark (DZGM)	1920	1923	3	
Soviet Khiva Ruble (SUVT)	1920	1923	3	
Memel Mark (MMLM)	1920	1923	3	
Canton Dollar (CNDC)	1935	1938	3	
Netherlands Indies Gumpyo Gulden (IDDJ)	1941	1944	3	Yes
Romania Infinex Leu (ROI)	1941	1944	3	Yes
Philippine Guerilla Peso (PHG)	1942	1945	3	
Malaya Gumpyo Dollar (MYAG)	1942	1945	3	Yes
Netherlands Indies Gumpyo Roepiah (NIDR)	1943	1946	3	
Nationalist Manchurian Yuan (CNNY)	1945	1948	3	
Japanese Allied Yen (JPA)	1945	1948	3	
German Allied Mark (DEA)	1945	1948	3	Yes

German Sperrmark (DES)	1951	1954	3	
Portuguese India Escudo (INPE)	1959	1962	3	
Reunion Franc (REF)	1959	1962	3	Yes
Katanga Franc (KATF)	1960	1963	3	
Viet Nam South Dong (VNS)	1975	1978	3	
Laos Liberation Kip (LAL)	1976	1979	3	Yes
Brazil Cruzado (BRC)	1986	1989	3	Yes
Nicaragua Cordoba (NIC)	1988	1991	3	Yes
Brazil Cruzeiro (BRE)	1990	1993	3	Yes
Russian Ruble (RUR)	1991	1994	3	
Bosnia New Dinar (BAN)	1994	1997	3	
Alabama Confederate Dollar (CSALD)	1861	1865	4	
Arkansas Confederate Dollar (CSAKD)	1861	1865	4	
Florida Confederate	1861	1865	4	

Dollar (CSFLD)				
Georgia Confederate Dollar (CSGAD)	1861	1865	4	
Louisiana Confederate Dollar (CSLAD)	1861	1865	4	
Mississippi Confederate Dollar (CSMSD)	1861	1865	4	
North Carolina Confederate Dollar (CSNCD)	1861	1865	4	
South Carolina Confederate Dollar (CSSCD)	1861	1865	4	
Tennessee Confederate Dollar (CSTND)	1861	1865	4	
Texas Confederate Dollar (CSTXD)	1861	1865	4	
Spanish Escudo (ESE)	1864	1868	4	
Yugoslav Kronen (YUK)	1918	1922	4	
Ruble Sovnazki (RUFS)	1918	1922	4	
Latvia Ruble (LVB)	1918	1922	4	Yes
Russian Ruble	1918	1922	4	Yes

Sovnazki (RUFS)				
Soviet Bukhara Ruble (BKSR)	1920	1924	4	
Germany Behelfszahlungsmittel (XDEB)	1940	1944	4	Yes
Nanking/CRB Yuan (CNPN)	1941	1945	4	
Burmese Gumpyo Rupee (BUG)	1941	1945	4	
Croatian Kuna (HRC)	1941	1945	4	
Hong Kong Military Yen (HKG)	1941	1945	4	
Philippine Gumpyo Peso (PHJ)	1941	1945	4	
Japanese Military Yen (XJPM)	1941	1945	4	Yes
French Indochina Military Yen (ICFG)	1941	1945	4	Yes
Oceania Gumpyo Pound (XOGP)	1941	1945	4	Yes
Serbian Dinar (SRDD)	1941	1945	4	Yes
New Hebrides	1941	1945	4	

Franc (NHF)				
French Franc (Allied Military Provisional) (FRP)	1944	1948	4	
Djibouti CFA Franc (DJC)	1945	1949	4	
Indonesia Guerilla Rupiah (IDG)	1945	1949	4	
Taiwan Nationalist Yuan (TWN)	1945	1949	4	Yes
German Bekomark	1954	1958	4	
German Libkamark	1954	1958	4	
Ruanda-Urundi Franc (BRIF)	1960	1964	4	
Algerian New Franc (DZF)	1960	1964	4	
Zambian Pound (ZMP)	1964	1968	4	
Congolese Zaire (CDZ)	1967	1971	4	
Croatian Dinar (HRD)	1991	1995	4	
Tatarstan Shamil (RUTS)	1992	1996	4	
Ethiopian Birr (ETB)	1993	1997	4	
Afghanistan	1998	2002	4	Yes

Dostumi Afghani (AFAD)				
Afghanistan Rabbini Afghani (AFAR)	1998	2002	4	Yes
Greek Phoenix (GRP)	1828	1833	5	
South African Republic Pound (ZAPP)	1905	1910	5	
Serbian Dinar (SRBD)	1913	1918	5	
Southwest Africa Mark (NAM)	1915	1920	5	
Ukraine Grivna (UAG)	1917	1922	5	
Rif Republic Riffan (MARR)	1921	1926	5	
Italian East Africa Lira (AOIL)	1936	1941	5	
Polish Cracow Zloty (PLK)	1940	1945	5	
Slovak Koruna (SKO)	1940	1945	5	
Netherlands Indies Gumpyo Roepiah (IDDR)	1941	1946	5	Yes
Indonesia "Java" Rupiah (IDJ)	1945	1950	5	
Indonesia	1945	1950	5	

"Nica" Guilder (IDD)				
Romanian New Leu (RON)	1947	1952	5	Yes
Chinese Old Jen Min Piao Yuan (CNP)	1948	1953	5	Yes
Bahraini Dinar (AED)	1971	1976	5	
Israel Shekel (ILL)	1980	1985	5	
Zairean New Zaire (ZRN)	1993	1998	5	Yes
Angola Kwanza Reajustado (AOR)	1995	2000	5	Yes
Tajikistan Ruble (TJR)	1995	2000	5	Yes
French Livre (Assignats) (FRL)	1789	1795	6	Yes
West Indies Joe (GYJ)	1830	1836	6	
Fiume Krone (FIUK)	1918	1924	6	
Estonia Marka (EEM)	1918	1924	6	Yes
Bohemia and Moravia Koruna (CSM)	1939	1945	6	
Japan Military Yen (CNPY)	1939	1945	6	Yes

Germany Reichskreditkassenscheine (XDEK)	1940	1946	6	
North Viet Nam Piastre Dong Viet (VDD)	1953	1959	6	Yes
Rhodesian Pound (RHP)	1964	1970	6	
Peru Inti (PEI)	1985	1991	6	Yes
Transnistrian Kupon Ruble (PDK)	1994	2000	6	Yes
Connecticut Continental Shilling (CCTS)	1776	1783	7	Yes
Delaware Continental Shilling (CDES)	1776	1783	7	Yes
Maryland Continental Shilling (CMDS)	1776	1783	7	Yes
Massachusetts Continental Shilling (CMAS)	1776	1783	7	Yes
New Jersey Continental Shilling (CNJS)	1776	1783	7	Yes
New York Continental Shilling (CNYS)	1776	1783	7	Yes

North Carolina Continental Shilling (CNCS)	1776	1783	7	Yes
Pennsylvania Continental Shilling (CPAS)	1776	1783	7	Yes
Rhode Island Continental Shilling (CRHS)	1776	1783	7	Yes
South Carolina Continental Shilling (CSCS)	1776	1783	7	Yes
Virginia Continental Shilling (CVAS)	1776	1783	7	Yes
Georgia Continental Shilling (CGAS)	1776	1783	7	
New Hampshire Continental Shilling (CNHS)	1776	1783	7	
Hungarian Korona (HUK)	1918	1925	7	Yes
Viet Minh Piastre Dong Viet (VDP)	1946	1953	7	
Congolese Republic Franc (CDG)	1960	1967	7	Yes
Gambia Pound (GMP)	1964	1971	7	
Malawi Pound (MWP)	1964	1971	7	

Qatar-Dubai Riyal (XQDR)	1966	1973	7	
Peseta Guineana (GQP)	1968	1975	7	
Viet Nam New Dong (VNN)	1978	1985	7	
Equatorial Guinea Franco (GQF)	1985	1992	7	
Argentina Austral (ARA)	1985	1992	7	Yes
Russian Federation Ruble (RUR)	1991	1998	7	Yes
Belarus New Ruble (BYB)	1994	2001	7	Yes
Massachusetts Shilling Middle Tenor (CMAM)	1741	1749	8	
Massachusetts Shilling New Tenor (CMAN)	1741	1749	8	
New Hampshire Lawful Shilling (CNHL)	1755	1763	8	
Chinese Paper Tael (CNTP)	1853	1861	8	
Montenegro Perper (MEP)	1910	1918	8	
Kiau Chau Dollar (JPY)	1914	1922	8	
Germany Darlenskasse	1914	1922	8	

Ost Mark (DEOM)				
Ottoman Empire Paper Lira (XOTL)	1914	1922	8	
Polish Marka (PLM)	1916	1924	8	
German Kreditsperrmark (DERK)	1931	1939	8	Yes
German Effektensperrmark (DERE)	1931	1939	8	Yes
Czechoslovak New Koruna (CSC)	1945	1953	8	
Irian Barat Rupiah (IDIR)	1963	1971	8	
Connecticut Dollar (CCTD)	1783	1792	9	
Delaware Dollar (CDED)	1783	1792	9	
Georgia Dollar (CGAD)	1783	1792	9	
Maryland Dollar (CMDD)	1783	1792	9	
Massachusetts Dollar (CMAD)	1783	1792	9	
New Hampshire Dollar (CNHD)	1783	1792	9	
New Jersey Dollar (CNJD)	1783	1792	9	

New York Dollar (CNYD)	1783	1792	9	
North Carolina Dollar (CNCD)	1783	1792	9	
Pennsylvania Dollar (CPAD)	1783	1792	9	
Rhode Island Dollar (CRHD)	1783	1792	9	
South Carolina Dollar (CSCD)	1783	1792	9	
Virginia Dollar (CVAD)	1783	1792	9	
Fiji Old Dollar (FJO)	1865	1874	9	
Peking/Tientsin/ Northern China/FRB Yuan (CNPP)	1935	1944	9	
Meng Chiang (Bank of Inner Mongolia) Yuan (CNPM)	1936	1945	9	
Sinkiang Yuan (CNSY)	1939	1948	9	Yes
German Registermark (XRDERM/DERR)	1939	1948	9	Yes
German Handelsperrmark (DERH)	1939	1948	9	Yes
German Reichskreditkass	1939	1948	9	Yes

enschein (XDEK)				
South Korean Hwan (KRH)	1953	1962	9	
Rhodesia and Nyasaland Federation Pound (RHFP)	1956	1965	9	
Liberian Liberty Dollars (LRDL)	1991	2000	9	
Texas Dollar (TXSD)	1836	1846	10	
Austro-Hungarian Monetary Union Gulden (XATG)	1857	1867	10	
Moldova Ducat (MDD)	1857	1867	10	
Colombia Peso (COP)	1905	1915	10	Yes
British Military Authority Lira (LYB)	1941	1951	10	Yes
Greek New Drachma (GRN)	1944	1954	10	Yes
India Haj Pilgrimage Rupee (XINP)	1950	1960	10	
Somali Somalo (SOIS)	1950	1960	10	
Bulgarian Socialist Lev (BGM)	1952	1962	10	

French Affars and Issas Franc (AIF)	1967	1977	10	
Rhodesian Dollar (RHD/ZWC)	1970	1980	10	
Angola Kwanza Novo (AON)	1990	2000	10	Yes
Angola Escudo Portuguese (AOE)	1914	1925	11	
Saar Franc (SAAF)	1919	1930	11	
Spanish Republican Peseta (ESPR)	1931	1942	11	
Persian Gulf Rupee (XPGR)	1959	1970	11	
Reunion Nouveau Franc (REN)	1963	1974	11	
Ekuele (Epkwele) Guineana (GQE)	1975	1986	11	
Liberian JJ Dollars (LRDJ)	1989	2000	11	
German Behelfszahlungsmittel fuer die Deutsche Wehrmacht (XDEB)	1936	1948	12	Yes
North Korea	1947	1959	12	Yes

People's Won (KPP)			
Albanian Lek Foreign Exchange Certificates (ALX)	1953	1965	12
Saint Pierre CFA Nouveau Franc (XCF)	1960	1972	12
Ghana Revalued Cedi (GHR)	1967	1979	12
New Hampshire Colonial Shilling (CNHC)	1763	1776	13
Rhode Island Colonial Shilling (CRHC)	1763	1776	13
Ecuador Peso (ECP)	1871	1884	13
Soviet Chervonetz (SUC)	1922	1935	13
Manchukuo Yuan (CNMY)	1932	1945	13
Netherlands New Guinea Guilder (NNGG)	1950	1963	13
Argentina Peso Ley 18.188 (ARL)	1970	1983	13

Iraqi "Swiss print" Kurdistan Dinar (IQDS)	1991	2004	13
South German Vereinsgulden (XDSG)	1857	1871	14
Venezuela Venezolano (VEV)	1873	1887	14
Soviet New Ruble (SUM)	1947	1961	14
Guinea Franc (GNI)	1958	1972	14
Nigerian Pound (NGP)	1959	1973	14
Somali Scellino (SOS)	1960	1974	14
Guinea Syli (GNS/GNE)	1972	1986	14
Angola Kwanza (AOK)	1977	1991	14
Connecticut Shilling New Tenor (CCTN)	1740	1755	15
Argentina Peso Fuerte (ARF)	1860	1875	15
Colombian Gold Peso (COG)	1871	1886	15
Crete Drachma (GKD)	1898	1913	15
East Africa Rupee (XEAR)	1905	1920	15

Burmese Rupee (BUR)	1937	1952	15	
French Antilles Franc (XNF)	1960	1975	15	
Chilean Escudo (CLE)	1960	1975	15	Yes
Sudanese Dinar (SDD)	1992	2007	15	Yes
US Paper Dollar (USP)	1862	1878	16	
Bulgarian Lev Srebro (BGS)	1904	1920	16	
Italian Somaliland Rupiah (SOIR)	1909	1925	16	
Saudi Arabian Riyal (SAA)	1916	1932	16	
Danzig Gulden (DZGG)	1923	1939	16	
German Rentenmark (DEN)	1923	1939	16	
Estonia Kroon (EEN)	1924	1940	16	
Saudi Sovereign Riyal (SAS)	1936	1952	16	
Southern Rhodesian Currency Board Pound (RHSP)	1940	1956	16	
Saint Pierre CFA Franc (XCFG)	1943	1959	16	Yes

Indonesia New Rupiah (IDN)	1949	1965	16	Yes
British Caribbean Territories (Eastern Group) Dollar (XBCD)	1951	1967	16	
Timor Escudo (TPE)	1959	1975	16	
US Continental Dollar (USC)	1775	1792	17	Yes
Spanish Real/Peso Duro (ESR)	1847	1864	17	
Puerto Rican Peso (PRS)	1881	1898	17	
Kiau Chau Dollar (KCHD)	1897	1914	17	
Shanghai Dollar (CNDA)	1914	1931	17	
Peking Dollar (CNDB)	1914	1931	17	
Hankow Dollar (CNDH)	1914	1931	17	
Kansu Dollar (CNDK)	1914	1931	17	
Kwangtung Dollar (CNDG)	1914	1931	17	
Manchurian Dollar (CNDM)	1914	1931	17	
Heilungkiang Tiao (CNHT)	1914	1931	17	

Kirin Tiao (CNKT)	1914	1931	17	
Shantung Dollar (CNDS)	1914	1931	17	
Szechwan Dollar (CNDZ)	1914	1931	17	
Chinese Soviet Yuan (CNSD)	1931	1948	17	
Italian States Franco (XITF)	1798	1816	18	
Riksdaler Riksmynt (SEM)	1855	1873	18	
Latvia Lat (LVA)	1922	1940	18	
Lithuanian Lita (LTB)	1922	1940	18	
Italian Lira (XITL)	1925	1943	18	
Chinese Custom Gold Units (CNU)	1930	1948	18	
Djibouti Franc (DJA)	1949	1967	18	
Angolan Escudo (AOS)	1958	1976	18	Yes
Uruguay Peso Nuevo (UYP/UYN)	1975	1993	18	Yes
South German Gulden (XDEG)	1838	1857	19	
North German	1838	1857	19	

Thaler (XDET)				
Albanian Lek (ALK)	1946	1965	19	
North Viet Nam New Dong (VDN/VNC)	1959	1978	19	
Brazil Cruzeiro Novo (BRB)	1967	1986	19	Yes
Congo CFA Franc (COF)	1973	1992	19	
Gabon CFA Franc (GAF)	1973	1992	19	
Chinese US Dollar Foreign Exchange Certificates (CNX)	1979	1998	19	
Czechoslovak Pre-War Koruna (CSO)	1919	1939	20	
Belgian Belga (BEB)	1925	1945	20	
Madagascar Franc (MGG)	1925	1945	20	
Libyan Pound (LYP)	1951	1971	20	
Cambodia Old Riel (KHO)	1955	1975	20	
South Viet Nam Republic Dong (VNR)	1955	1975	20	Yes
Bulgarian Lev Foreign	1966	1986	20	

Currency	Start	End	Years	Exchange Certificates (BGX)
Luxembourg Convertible Franc (LUC)	1970	1990	20	
Guinea-Bissau Peso (GWP)	1976	1996	20	
New Hampshire Shilling New Tenor (CNHN)	1742	1763	21	
Connecticut Colonial Shilling (CCTC)	1755	1776	21	
Russian Gold Ruble (RUER)	1897	1918	21	
Albania Franga (ALF)	1925	1946	21	
Hungarian Pengoe (HUP)	1925	1946	21	Yes
Laos Old Kip (LAO)	1955	1976	21	
Ghana Pound (GHP)	1958	1979	21	
Uganda Shilling (UGS/UGW)	1966	1987	21	Yes
Mali Franc (MLF/MAF)	1962	1984	22	
Zairean Zaire (ZRZ)	1971	1993	22	Yes
Luxembourg Thaler (LUT)	1848	1871	23	

Yugoslav Serbian Dinar (YUS)	1918	1941	23	
Mozambique Libra Esterlina (MZL)	1919	1942	23	
Tanu Tuva Aksha (TVAA)	1921	1944	23	
Soviet Gold Ruble (SUG)	1924	1947	23	
Palestine Pound (PSP)	1927	1950	23	
Bolivian Peso (BOP)	1963	1986	23	Yes
Brazil Mil Reis (BRM)	1822	1846	24	Yes
Central American Escudo (XCAE)	1823	1847	24	
Sinkiang Tael (CNST)	1912	1936	24	
Yunnan Yuan (CNYY)	1912	1936	24	
Austria Old Schilling (ATO)	1923	1947	24	
German Reichsmark (DER)	1924	1948	24	Yes
Yugoslav Hard Dinar (YUD)	1966	1990	24	Yes
Paper Riksdaler Banco (SEO)	1830	1855	25	

Austro-Hungarian Gulden (ATG)	1867	1892	25	
Colombia Paper Peso (COB)	1880	1905	25	Yes
Malaya Dollar (MYAD)	1938	1963	25	
South Yemeni Dinar (YDD)	1965	1990	25	
Austro-Hungarian Kronen (ATK)	1892	1918	26	Yes
Massachusetts Colonial Shilling (CMAC)	1749	1776	27	
German East African Rupie (DOAR)	1890	1917	27	
Maryland Colonial New Shilling (CMDN)	1748	1776	28	
North Carolina Shilling New Tenor (CNCN)	1748	1776	28	
South Carolina Colonial Shilling (CSCC)	1748	1776	28	
Zanzibar Rupee (ZZR)	1908	1936	28	
Lebanon-Syria Pound (XLSP)	1920	1948	28	

New Jersey Colonial Shilling (CNJC)	1746	1776	30
Haiti Silver Gourde (HTS)	1814	1844	30
British West Indies Dollar (XBWD)	1935	1965	30
Madagascar and Comores CFA Franc (XMCF)	1945	1975	30
Polish US Dollar Foreign Exchange Certificates (PLX)	1960	1990	30
Soviet Hard Ruble (SUR)	1961	1991	30
Rhode Island Proclamation Shilling (CRHP)	1709	1740	31
Rhode Island Shilling New Tenor (CRHN)	1740	1771	31
Guyana British West Indies Dollar (XBWD)	1935	1966	31
Ethiopian Dollar (ETD)	1945	1976	31
French Indochina Piastre of Commerce (ICFC)	1863	1895	32

Cameroon Mark (CMDM)	1884	1916	32	
Angola Angolar (AOA)	1926	1958	32	
Israel Pound (ILP)	1948	1980	32	
COMECON Transferable Ruble (XTR)	1960	1992	32	
Tunisian Franc (TNF)	1858	1891	33	Yes
Colombia Peso Oro (COE)	1837	1871	34	
Mozambique Mil Reis (MZR)	1877	1911	34	
Maldive Islands Rupee (MVP/MVQ)	1947	1981	34	
Somalia Shilling (SOS)	1960	1994	34	Yes
Korea Yen (KROY)	1910	1945	35	
New Hebrides CFP Franc (NHF)	1945	1981	36	
North Korea Foreign Won (KPX)	1959	1995	36	
Dutch Gulden (BRG)	1624	1661	37	
Burmese Kyat (BUK)	1952	1989	37	

Bulgarian Heavy Lev (BGL/BGK)	1962	1999	37	Yes
Haiti Piastre Gourde (HTT)	1776	1814	38	
Union Latine Franc (XULF)	1889	1927	38	
Union Latine Lira (XULL)	1889	1927	38	
Ethiopian Silver Talari (ETT)	1893	1931	38	
Netherlands Indies Gumpyo Gulden (NIDJ)	1905	1943	38	
Djibouti Franc Germinal (DJG)	1907	1945	38	
North Carolina Proclamation Shilling (CNCP)	1709	1748	39	
Rial Hassani (MAH)	1881	1920	39	
Tibet Silver Rupee (TBR)	1912	1951	39	
Finland New Markka (FIM)	1963	2002	39	
Paraguay Paper Peso (PYP)	1903	1943	40	Yes
Czechoslovak Hard Koruna (CSK)	1953	1993	40	
French Franc (FRF)	1962	2002	40	

Currency	Start	End	Value
Georgia Colonial Shilling (CGAC)	1735	1776	41
Philippine Peso Fuerte (PHF)	1857	1898	41
Ottoman Empire Gold Lira (XOTG)	1881	1922	41
South African Pound (ZAP)	1920	1961	41
Sudanese Pound (SDP)	1957	1998	41
Malagasy Franc (MGF)	1963	2004	41
Maryland Proclamation Shilling (CMDP)	1709	1751	42
Italian States Ducat (XITD)	1818	1860	42
Peru Peso (PEP)	1821	1863	42
DDR Ostmark (DDM)	1948	1990	42
East Caribbean Dollar (XCD)	1965	2008	43
Sao Tome and Principe Mil Reis (STM)	1869	1913	44
Bulgarian Lev Zlato (BGZ)	1880	1924	44
Tangier Franco	1912	1956	44

(MATF)				
Polish Heavy Zloty (PLZ)	1950	1994	44	Yes
South Carolina Proclamation Shilling (CSCP)	1703	1748	45	
Massachusetts Old Tenor Proclamation Shilling (CMAP)	1704	1749	45	
Cape Verde Mil Reis (CVM)	1869	1914	45	Yes
Serbian Dinar (SRBD)	1873	1918	45	
Finland Markka (FIN)	1917	1962	45	Yes
Tonga Pound Sterling (TOS)	1921	1966	45	
Brazil Cruzeiro (BRZ)	1942	1987	45	Yes
Connecticut Shilling Old Tenor (CCTO)	1709	1755	46	
Argentina National Peso (XARP)	1816	1862	46	Yes
Hawaii Dollar (HWD)	1847	1893	46	
Afghanistan Kabuli Rupee (AFR)	1881	1927	46	
French West	1895	1941	46	

African Franc (XAOF)				
East Africa Shilling (XEAS)	1921	1967	46	
Haiti Paper Gourde (HTP)	1826	1873	47	
Luxembourg Mark (LUM)	1871	1918	47	
New Caledonia CFP Franc (NCF)	1945	1992	47	
Costa Rican Peso (CRP)	1848	1896	48	
South Korean Old Won (KRO)	1905	1953	48	Yes
Greek Drachma (GRD)	1954	2002	48	
North German Vereinsthaler (XDNT)	1857	1907	50	
Yugoslav Federation Dinar (YUF)	1945	1995	50	Yes
Chinese Silver Yin Yuan (CNS)	1949	2000	51	
Paraguay Peso Fuerte (PYF)	1871	1923	52	
Scandinavian Monetary Union Krona (XSMK)	1872	1924	52	
Trinidad and Tobago Dollar (TTO)	1899	1951	52	

Fiji Pound (FJP)	1917	1969	52	
Delaware Colonial Shilling (CDEC)	1723	1776	53	
Italian States Lira Austriaca (XITA)	1813	1866	53	
German Mark (DEP)	1871	1924	53	Yes
British West Africa Pound	1913	1966	53	
Western Samoa Pound (WSP)	1914	1967	53	
New Hampshire Old Tenor Proclamation Shilling (CNHP)	1709	1763	54	Yes
Riksdaler Specie (SES)	1776	1830	54	
Paper Riksdaler (SER)	1776	1830	54	
Argentina Gold Peso (ARG)	1875	1929	54	
Taiwan Yen (TWY)	1895	1949	54	
Maltese Pound (MTP)	1914	1968	54	
German Deutsche Mark (DEM)	1948	2002	54	
Austria (New) Schilling (ATS)	1947	2002	55	

Italian States Scudo (XITS)	1814	1870	56
Bermuda Pound (BMP)	1914	1970	56
Paraguay National Peso (PYN)	1813	1870	57
French Oceania (Tahiti) Franc (PFG)	1888	1945	57
Australian Pound (AUP)	1909	1966	57
Montenegro Krone (MEK)	1852	1910	58
Chinese Dollar/Yuan (Chungking/Shanghai Yuan) (CND)	1890	1948	58
Mozambique Escudo (MZE)	1922	1980	58
Union Latine Drachma (XULD)	1868	1927	59
Union Latine Peseta (XULP)	1868	1927	59
Danish Rigsbankdaler (DKR)	1813	1873	60
Greenland Riksbankdaler (GLR)	1813	1873	60
New Zealand	1907	1967	60

Pound (NZP)				
Dominican Republic Silver Peso (DOS)	1844	1905	61	
British North Borneo Dollar (BNBD)	1885	1946	61	
Massachusetts Bay Shilling (CMAB)	1642	1704	62	
Union Latine Franc (XULF)	1865	1927	62	
Union Latine Franc (XULF)	1865	1927	62	
Union Latine Franc (XULF)	1865	1927	62	
Union Latine Lira (XULL)	1865	1927	62	
Portuguese Guinea Escudo (GWE)	1914	1976	62	
Iceland Old Krone (ISJ)	1918	1980	62	Yes
Timor Pataca (TPP)	1895	1958	63	
Sao Tome and Principe Escudo (STE)	1914	1977	63	
Andorra Pesseta (ADP)	1936	1999	63	
Suriname Guilder (SRG)	1940	2003	63	Yes

New Jersey Proclamation Shilling (CNJP)	1682	1746	64	
Jamaica Pound (JMP)	1905	1969	64	
Danish West Indies Rigsdaler (DWIR)	1784	1849	65	
Nicaragua Silver Peso (NIP)	1847	1912	65	
Mauritius Dollar (MUD)	1810	1876	66	
New York Proclamation Shilling (CNYP)	1709	1776	67	
Pennsylvania Proclamation Dollar (CPAP)	1709	1776	67	
Virginia Proclamation Shilling (CVAP)	1709	1776	67	
New Caledonia Franc Germinal (NCG)	1874	1941	67	
Danish West Indies Dalare (DWID)	1849	1917	68	
Luxembourg Gulden (LUG)	1848	1918	70	
Argentina Paper Peso Moneda National (ARM)	1899	1970	71	Yes
Portuguese	1931	2002	71	

Account Conto (PTC)				
El Salvador Peso (SVP)	1847	1919	72	
Bulgarian Lev (BGO)	1879	1952	73	Yes
Vatican City Lira (VAL)	1929	2002	73	
Russian Assignatzia (RUEA)	1768	1843	75	
Russian Silver Ruble (RUES)	1839	1914	75	
Russian Paper Ruble (RUEP)	1843	1918	75	
Belgian Congo Franc (CBEF)	1885	1960	75	
Afghanistan Afghani (AFA)	1927	2002	75	Yes
Madeira Islands Milreis (IPM)	1834	1910	76	
Portuguese Mil Reis (PTM)	1835	1911	76	
Nicaragua Gold Cordoba (NIG)	1912	1988	76	Yes
Ceylon Rupee (LNR)	1872	1949	77	
Guatemala Peso (GTP)	1847	1925	78	
Portuguese India Rupia (INPR)	1881	1959	78	
Moroccan Franc	1881	1959	78	Yes

(MAF)				
Colombia Peso Oro (COP)	1915	1993	78	Yes
Honduras Peso (HNP)	1847	1926	79	
Romania Silver Leu (ROS)	1867	1947	80	Yes
British Honduras Dollar (BZH)	1894	1974	80	
Irish Pound (IEP)	1922	2002	80	
Sarawak Dollar (SWKD)	1863	1946	83	
Turkish Lira (TRL)	1922	2005	83	Yes
German States Convention Thaler (XDCT)	1753	1838	85	
Straits Settlements Dollar (STSD)	1857	1946	89	
Portuguese Escudo (PTE)	1911	2002	91	
Pound Sterling (CAP)	1766	1858	92	
Reunion Franc Germinal (REG)	1851	1944	93	
Hyderabad Sicca Rupee (INRH)	1858	1951	93	
French Indochina	1862	1955	93	

Piastre (ICFP)				
Newfoundland Dollar (NFLD)	1858	1952	94	
Greenland Krone (GLK)	1873	1967	94	
Polish Zloty (XPLZ)	1700	1795	95	
Taiwan Tael/Dollar (TWT)	1800	1895	95	
Portuguese Guinea Mil Reis (GWM)	1879	1974	95	
Bahamas Pound (BSP)	1869	1966	97	
Russian Empire Paper Ruble (RUEP)	1818	1917	99	
Bolivia Boliviano (BOL)	1863	1962	99	Yes
Danish Rigsdaler Courant (DKC)	1713	1813	100	
Austro-Hungarian Convention Gulden (XATC)	1753	1857	104	
East India Rix Dollar (XEIR)	1800	1905	105	
Manx Pound (IMP)	1865	1971	106	
Iranian Kran	1825	1932	107	

(IRK)				
Franc Guiana (GUF)	1851	1959	108	
Guadeloupe Franc (GPF)	1851	1959	108	
Martinique Franc (MQF)	1851	1959	108	
Algerian Franc Germinal (DZG)	1851	1959	108	Yes
Chilean Peso/Condor (CLC)	1851	1959	108	Yes
Daler Silvermynt (SED)	1665	1776	111	
Greek Silver Drachma (GRS)	1833	1944	111	Yes
Uruguay Peso Fuerte (UYF)	1862	1975	113	Yes
Paper Daler (SEP)	1661	1776	115	
Ecuador Sucre (ECS)	1884	2000	116	
Luxembourg Financial Franc (LUL)	1870	1991	121	
Monaco Franc Germinal (MCG)	1837	1959	122	
Peru Sol (PES/PEH)	1863	1985	122	Yes
Silver	1700	1823	123	

Piastre/Peso (XESE)				
Brazil Reis (BRD)	1694	1822	128	Yes
Thailand Silver Tical (THT)	1800	1928	128	
Netherlands East Indies Guilder (IDDG)	1817	1945	128	
Jersey Pound Sterling (JEP)	1840	1971	131	
Spanish Peseta (ESP)	1868	2002	134	
Italian States Scudo Romano (XITS)	1700	1835	135	
Colonial Shilling (XCCS)	1640	1776	136	
San Marino Lira (SML)	1865	2001	136	
Venezuela Bolivar (VEB)	1871	2008	137	Yes
East India Company Dollar (XEID)	1719	1858	139	
Austrian Paper Gulden (ATP)	1753	1892	139	
Italian Lira (ITL)	1862	2002	140	
Newfoundland Pound (NFLP)	1713	1858	145	
Bukhara Tenga	1768	1920	152	

(BKHT) Portuguese Reis (PRT)	1505	1658	153	
Luxembourg Franc (LUF)	1848	2002	154	
French Franc Germinal/Franc Poincare (FRG)	1803	1959	156	Yes
Azores Milreis (APM)	1750	1911	161	
Ceylon Rijksdaalder (Rix Dollar) (XNLR)	1658	1821	163	
French Colonial Livre (XFCL)	1654	1820	166	
Mexico Silver Peso (MXP)	1822	1992	170	Yes
Belgian Franc (BEF)	1831	2002	171	
Tibet Tangka (TBT)	1735	1912	177	
Poland Florin Zloty (PLF)	1614	1795	181	
Portuguese Reis (PTR)	1722	1911	189	Yes
Netherlands Guilder (NLG)	1813	2002	189	
Danish Gold Krone of Account (DKG)	1513	1713	200	
French India	1736	1954	218	

Roupie (INFR)				
Scotland Pound (SSP)	1707	1971	264	
Northern Irish Pound (IBP)	1694	1971	277	
Korea Won (KROW)	1625	1910	285	
Italian States Testone (XITT)	1500	1814	314	
Iranian Toman (IRT)	1600	1932	332	
Mexican Trade Silver Dollar (XMSD)	1600	1935	335	
Chinese Silver Tael (CNT)	1600	1935	335	Yes
Hamburg Schilling (HAMS)	1510	1871	361	
Ottoman Empire Piastre (XOTP)	1463	1881	418	
Italian States Lira (XITL)	1284	1862	578	
French Livre Tournois (FRT)	1204	1795	591	Yes

What this tells us is that people almost always will lose faith in Fiat currency, especially when governments/banks have the power to print to make themselves wealthy or go to war and destroying our livelihoods. That is why Fiat currencies and Fractional reserve banking are crimes against humanity.

Fiat Currencies Currently on Death Row:

Currency Name (Currency Code)	Inception	Duration
Venezuela Bolivar Fuerte	2008	7 mos.
Sudanese Pound (SDG)	2007	1
Turkish New Lira (TRY)	2005	3
Suriname Dollar (SRD)	2004	4
Afghanistan Afghani (AFN)	2002	6
Yugoslav Noviy (Super) Dinar (SCD)	2002	6
Transnistrian New Ruble (PDN)	2001	7
Belarus Newer Ruble (BYR)	2000	8
Tajikistan Somoni (TJS)	2000	8
Angola Kwanza (new) (AOA)	1999	9
Bulgarian New Lev (BGN)	1999	9
Euro (EUR)	1999	9
Russian Federation New Ruble (RUB)	1999	9
Congolese Franc (CDF)	1998	10
Eritrean Nakfa (ERN)	1997	11
Ukraine Hryvnia (UAH)	1996	12
Bosnia Convertible Mark (BAM)	1995	13
Georgia Larit (GEL)	1995	13
Polish New Zloty (PLN)	1995	13
Serbian Dinar (RSD)	1994	14
Brazil Real (BRL)	1994	14
Croatian Kuna (HRK)	1994	14

Cuba "Peso Convertible" (CUC)	1994	14
Yugoslav Noviy (Super) Dinar (YUM)	1994	14
Somaliland Shilling (SQS)	1994	14
Uzbekistan Sum (UZS)	1994	14
Armenian Dram (AMD)	1993	15
Azerbaijan Manat (AZM)	1993	15
Colombia Peso (COP)	1993	15
Czech Koruna (CZK)	1993	15
Kazakhstan Tenge (KZT)	1993	15
Kyrgyzstan Som (KGS)	1993	15
Latvia Lat (LVL)	1993	15
Lithuania Lita (LTL)	1993	15
Macedonian New Denar (MKD)	1993	15
Mexico New Peso (MXN)	1993	15
Moldovan Leu (MDL)	1993	15
Myanmark Dollar Foreign Exchange Certificates (MMX)	1993	15
Namibia Dollar (NAD)	1993	15
Turkmenistan Manat (TMM)	1993	15
Uruguay Peso Uruguayo (UYU)	1993	15
Argentina Peso Convertible (ARS)	1992	16
Estonia Kroon (EEK)	1992	16
Slovak Koruna (SKK)	1992	16
Slovenia Tolar (SIT)	1992	16

Nicaragua Cordoba Oro (NIO)	1991	17
Peru Sol Nuevo (PE	1991	17
Yemeni Rial (YER)	1990	18
Myanmar Kyat (MMK)	1989	19
Bolivian Boliviano (New) (BOB)	1987	21
Cook Islands Dollar (CKD)*	1987	21
Uganda New Shilling (UGX)	1987	21
Aruba Guilder (AWG)	1986	22
New Franc Guineen (GNF)	1986	22
Israel New Shekel (ILS)	1985	23
Viet Nam Dong (VND)	1985	23
Madagascar Ariary (MGA)	1983	25
Iceland Krona (ISK)	1981	27
Maldive Islands Rufiyaa (MVR)	1981	27
Vanuatu Vatu (VUV)	1981	27
Mozambique Metical (MZM)	1980	28
Cambodia New Riel (KHR)	1980	28
Lesotho (Ma)Loti (LSL)	1980	28
Zimbabwe Dollar (ZWD)	1980	28
Ghana New Cedi (GHC)	1979	29
Laos New Kip (LAK)	1979	29
Sri Lanka Rupee (LKR)	1978	30
Djibouti Franc (DJF)	1977	31
Sao Tome and Principe Dobra (STD)	1977	31

Currency	Year	Value
Solomon Islands Dollar (SBD)	1977	31
Botswana Pula (BWP)	1976	32
Ethiopian Birr (ETB)	1976	32
Chilean Peso (CLP)	1975	33
Comoros Franc (KMF)	1975	33
Papua New Guinea Kina (PGK)	1975	33
Belize Dollar (BZD)	1974	34
Bhutan Ngultrum (BTN)	1974	34
Somali Shilin Soomaali (SOS)	1974	34
Swaziland Lilangeni (SZL)	1974	34
Barbados Dollar (BBD)	1973	35
Mauritania Ouguiya (MRO)	1973	35
Nigerian Naira (NGN)	1973	35
Qatari Rial (QAR)	1973	35
United Arab Emirates Dirham (AED)	1973	35
Bangladesh Taka (BDT)	1972	36
Rial Omani (OMR)	1972	36
Cayman Islands Dollar (KYD)	1971	37
Gambia Dalasi (GMD)	1971	37
Northern Irish Pound (IBP)	1971	37
Libyan Dinar (LYD)	1971	37
Malawi Kwacha (MWK)	1971	37
Scotland Pound (SSP)	1971	37
Bermudan Dollar (BMD)	1970	38

Fiji Dollar (FJD)	1969	39
Jamaica Dollar (JMD)	1969	39
Maltese Lira (MTL)	1968	40
Zambian Kwacha (ZMK)	1968	40
Brunei Dollar (BND)	1967	41
New Zealand Dollar (NZD)	1967	41
Western Samoa Ta'la (WST)	1967	41
Singapore Dollar (SGD)	1967	41
Australian Dollar (AUD)	1966	42
Bahamas Dollar (BSD)	1966	42
Kenyan Shilling (KES)	1966	42
Tanzania Shilling (TZS)	1966	42
Tonga Pa'anga (TOP)	1966	42
Albanian "Heavy" Lek (ALL)	1965	43
Bahraini Dinar (BHD)	1965	43
Indonesian Rupiah (IDR)	1965	43
Algerian Dinar (DZD)	1964	44
Burundi Franc (BIF)	1964	44
Rwanda Franc (RWF)	1964	44
Sierra Leone Leone (SLL)	1964	44
Malaysian Ringgit (MYR)	1963	45
South Korean Won (KRW)	1962	46
Kuwaiti Dinar (KWD)	1961	47
South African Rand (ZAR)	1961	47
Franc Metropolitan (XMF)	1960	48
Tunisian Dinar (TND)	1960	48
North Korea New Won	1959	49

(KPW)		
Moroccan Dirham (MAD)	1959	49
Tunisian Dinar (TND)	1958	50
French Polynesian CFP Franc (XPF)	1957	51
Chinese Renminbi Yuan (CNY)	1953	55
Romanian Leu (RON)	1952	56
Saudi Riyal (SAR)	1952	56
Jordan Dinar (JOD)	1950	58
Faeroe Islands Kronur (FOK)	1949	59
Taiwan New Dollar (TWD)	1949	59
Lebanese Pound (LBP)	1948	60
Pakistan Rupee (PKR)	1948	60
Syrian Pound (SYP)	1948	60
Dominican Republic Peso Oro (DOP)	1947	61
Hungary Forint (HUF)	1946	62
Liberian Dollar (LRD)	1944	64
Paraguay Guarani (PYG)	1943	65
West African CFA Franc (XOF)	1941	67
Central African CFA Franc (XAF)	1941	67
Mauritius Rupee (MUR)	1934	74
Nepalese Rupee (NPR)	1933	75
Iranian Rial (IRR)	1932	76
Iraqi Dinar (IQD)	1931	77

Currency	Year	Value
Thailand Baht (THB)	1928	80
Gibraltar Pound (GIP)	1713	81
Honduras Lempira (HNL)	1926	82
Guatemala Quetzal (GTQ)	1925	83
Liechtenstein Franc (LIF)*	1921	87
El Salvador Colon (SVC)	1919	89
Guyana Dollar (GYD)	1916	92
Mongolia Tugrik (MNT)	1915	93
Cape Verde Escudo (CVE)	1914	94
Cyprus Pound (CYP)	1914	94
Falkland Islands Pound (FKP)	1908	100
French Pacific Territories Franc (XPF)	1905	103
Norway Krone (NOK)	1905	103
Somali N-Shilling (SON)	1905	103
Trinidad and Tobago Dollar (TTD)	1905	103
Panama Balboa (PAB)	1903	105
Macao Pataca (MOP)	1901	107
Saint Helena Pound (SHP)	1901	107
Seychelles Rupee (SCR)	1900	108
Philippine Piso (PHP)	1898	110
Costa Rican Colon (CRC)	1896	112
Hong Kong Dollar (HKD)	1895	113
Egyptian Pound (EGP)	1885	123
Danish Krone (DKK)	1873	135
Swedish Krona (SEK)	1873	135

Currency	Year	Value
Haiti Gourde (HTG)	1872	136
Japanese Yen (JPY)	1871	137
Cuban Peso (CUP)	1859	149
Canadian Dollar (CAD)	1858	150
Guernsey Pound Sterling (GGP)	1827	181
India Rupee (INR)	1823	185
Netherlands Antillan Guilder (ANG)	1821	187
Swiss Franc (CHF)	1799	209
US Dollar (USD)	**1792**	**216**
Pound Sterling (GBP)	1694	314

After looking at these charts, I can find one fail at the end of this chart (see the bold letters above). The US Dollar has not been alive since 1792. There have been different types of currencies in the US and 2 other US central banks. The US Dollar has only been alive since the late 1800s. Between 1792 to the late 1800s, there have been 2 gold/silver backed currencies and 2 fiat currencies. None of them has been called the US Dollar!

Chapter Two
Papered Over: The Worthless History of Fiat Paper Currencies almost 1000 year reign

The time period of almost 1000 years of existence of creation of currency by governments and bankers is laden with destruction of wealth and lives around the world! Here are some stories that caused big events and were not reported as reckless behaviour by governments and bankers. We may never get the truth behind money crisis, but here are some of the biggest stories:

China's first paper currencies

I thought the inventor of fiat paper money should get the spotlight as the 4 charts that I would now show you will clearly make you understand that a fiat currency with no limitation attached ends in failure together with the empires printing them, whether modern or old.

The four different empires from the Sung Government, the inventors of Fiat Currency, to the Yuan Dynasty- they all had the same faith. They started with currency redeemable in coin that over time was debased and after 5-6 decades turned into a full non-backed currency and that is when people lost faith in fake currency created either by privately-owned banks or governments.

They started trading in other commodities, mostly silver and silk. The currency declined very quickly as government revenue shrank and they had to print money or start a war to print more money to pay for government expenses and welfare. A middle class emerged before the end as the printing made people "wealthy" for a while, but soon after their newly acquired wealth of paper money started rapidly decreasing in value. At the end when people stopped using it, massive issuance of new money fed the currency's decline and led to the end of an empire/government.

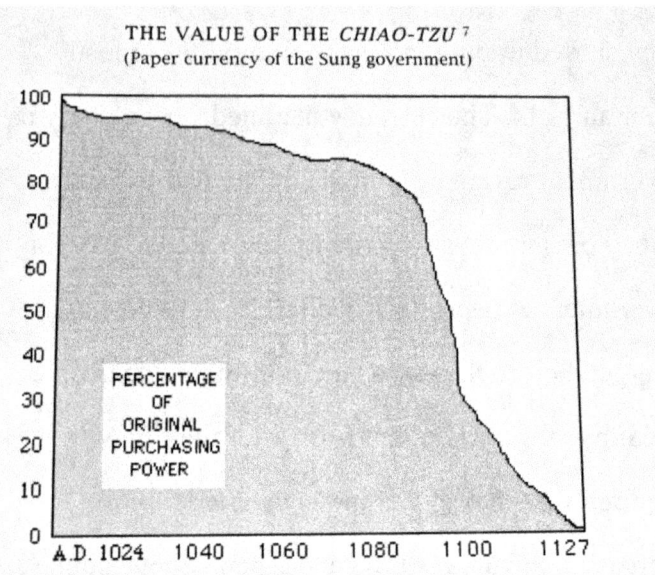

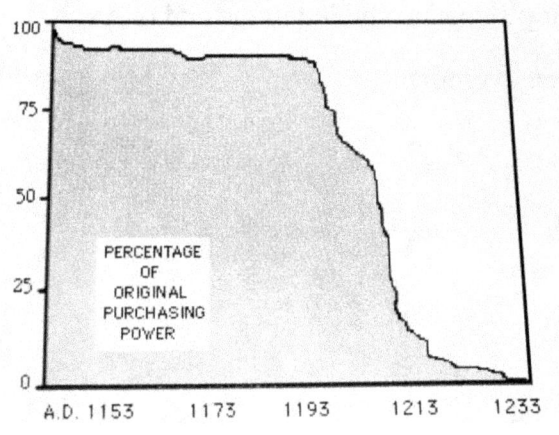

---

[3] Charts from The History of Fiat Paper Money by Ralph T. Foster

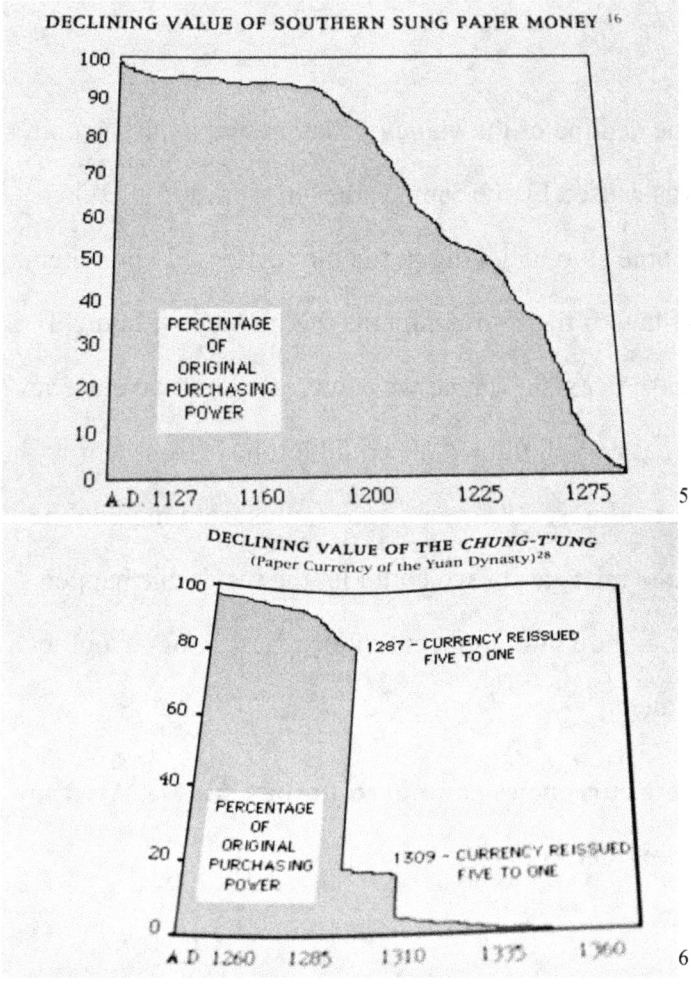

[4] Charts from The History of Fiat Paper Money by Ralph T. Foster

[5] Charts from The History of Fiat Paper Money by Ralph T. Foster

[6] Charts from The History of Fiat Paper Money by Ralph T. Foster

The decline of the value of Fiat money in all 4 empires was caused by the same forces in work today. When people stop believing in the money forced upon them by law of their governments that money will quickly cease to exist. Maybe we can create our own currency? What do you think? We could let the lessons learnt from almost 1000 years ago stop us from making the same mistakes or we could let the inevitable happen - the failure of our current monetary system on a global scale.

New currencies compared to the Chinese. Are they doing better?

---

[7] Source http://www.shadowstats.com

Source: Aluminium Price - U.S. Bureau of Mines and the U.S. Geological Survey-Minerals Yearbook (MYB) and its predecessor, Mineral Resources of the United States (MR), and Metal Prices in the United States through 1998 (MP98) www.http://minerals.usgs.gov/ds/2005/140/
US Inflation: Consumer Price Index (Estimate) 1800-2008. Handbook of Labor Statistics, U.S. Department of Labor
UK Inflation: Inflation: the Value of the Pound 1750-2005. Research Paper 06/09, House of Commons Library, UK, 13 February 2006

Unlimited National Debt in Austria

The start of our current Keysian economic system of the Government borrowing money has been around for over 300 years. The first place it appears in the history books is in Austria. Its founder was The First Bank of Austria. This bank's sole purpose was to fund public debt by keeping deposits in the bank and then lending them out. This bank didn't last for long and failed miserably when people caught up to the scheme.

In 1759, Count Sinzendorff, an Austrian official and financier invented bailouts. Count Sinzendorff, who had recklessly borrowed money, created a bank where the taxpayers would need to deposit their money. This allowed the government to borrow the tax payer's deposits. This put the Sinzendorff out of harm's way and the citizens on the hook for debt they never borrowed. This strategy is the precursor for today's Keynesian economic system where it is believed that governments can borrow more and more money to pay off old debt. This would be comparable to you taking out credit card then maxing it out, only to get a new credit card to pay the interest on your first credit card, that is until the second one is maxed out, and then you get a third card and continuing this process for eternity.

The first FIAT paper notes worked just like today's bonds and had interest attached to them. They were so impressed with the expansion of business in the country that soon after issuing the first bonds, they issued a second round. The second issue was borrowed in 1769 and then a third was borrowed rather quickly in 1771. The first thought was that this created prosperity due to the increase in commerce and wealth of the initial issue of bonds. The next two lasted for very short periods of time and more bonds and money had to be issued quickly until people lost their wealth and faith in the Austrian currency in 1797. But they didn't stop there like the US and many other countries of today. Austria doubled down and went to wars. That led to the creation of more bond issues and uncontrolled government expenditure.

In the end, the Austrian currency had lost over 90% of its value.

However, this idea was welcomed in other European countries where Kings and Queens had to tax their people in order to go to wars and buy things. So, they took to the strategy of today's government of issuing bonds and printing currency.

This idea of stealing from the public by inflation was a much better approach for hated kings and queens as their peasants would not see what would happen until it was too late!

In 1679 King William racked up the English National debt to 21.5 million Pounds in order to finance a war. The King paid back only 5.1 million Pounds during peace time. At the End of the Napoleonic Wars in 1816 the public debt was 773.1 million Pounds, and only 44.5 million paid back to the banks.

See the chart below.

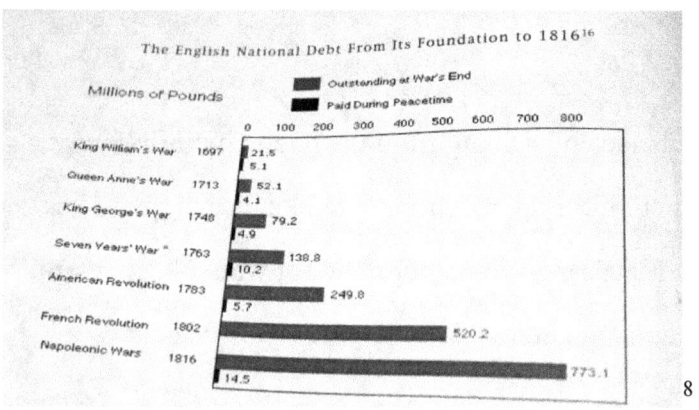

[8]

The bankers that issue this kind of money always win!!!

---

[8] Charts from The History of Fiat Paper Money by Ralph T. Foster

The Ottoman Empire

The Devaluation of the Ottoman Akçe currency: Ottoman Akçe was replaced by the Kuruş (1 kurus = 120 akçe), with the para (1/40 kurus) as a subunit. The Kurus, in turn, later became a subdivision of the Lira. This leads us to the next crime of Fiat Currencies Devaluation and Inflation as the Akçe was replaced 1 to 120 by a new currency but the value of the new currency was basically the same. The End of the Ottoman Empire shows the power of debasing a currency. Here is a picture of Ottoman Currency through its history of debasement.

As you can see this is very similar to the devaluations of the Bulgarian Leva, Russian Ruble, Argentinian Peso and the French Assignate mentioned below.

The Mississippi Bubble and the French Revolution

The French revolution is well known from big movie productions like *Les Miserables*, but this movie misses out on the most important cause of the French revolution, which is the devaluation and mass printing of the French Currency, the Assignate. The Assignate were printed to a point when people could not afford to buy food. Thereby you get the French revolution and thus the movie and musical *Les Miserables*.

Within 70 years the currency collapsed twice. The first experiment on French soil started in 1715.

John Law and the Mississippi Bubble

In 1715, France had recently lost a war. The monarchy was looking at a massive loss as expenses were double of the current income. John Law, the current head of Banque Generale, came up with the idea of issuing bank notes. He issued banknotes (the first issue) and bought the Mississippi Company. Then he started to issue shares in the Mississippi Company. The shares of the Mississippi Company jumped due to the purchase and the first step towards a bubble started. In 1718, Banque Generale became Banque Royale and started issuing more bank notes and more shares in the Mississippi Company. The economy boomed and people felt wealthy like never before. In 1720, John Law became minister of finance in France. The same year the value of the shares in the Mississippi Company popped, but the way John Law got out of bankruptcy was by issuing more bank notes in order to prop up the stock price. State pensions were forcibly invested in the company to keep it afloat. This didn't work. As paper notes now traded to a discount vs. silver coins, people started hoarding silver as the value of the bank notes dropped further.

A few months later the shares in the Mississippi Company were held by almost anyone in France. Then some elites got the news that the shares might lose all their value. A bank run started as people fled from the monetary hills into gold and silver to protect their wealth from total demolition. This was one of the first bank runs written about in history. Then the bubble popped and both the bank notes and the shares become completely worthless and people lost all that they had saved up. If you wanted to insult someone at the time you'd call them a banker. People got thrown in jail for using gold and silver, but this didn't stop people from buying. In the end, bankers died like flies as the guillotine worked overtime to restore justice.

The French lost all their faith in this new paper money for a generation at least.

THE ASSIGNATE AND THE FRENCH REVOLUTION

70 years later, after the revolution that swept the country the French Government was deeply in debt. The idea of issuing paper money to pay back some of the debt sprung up. The current finance minister of the time Necker warned that printing money would only lead to a new Mississippi Bubble! Necker strongly refused to participate in printing money out of thin air, but the assemble came up with the idea of confiscating the Vatican's property and use the Assignate to sell the property off. The one-time issue of 400M livre was debated for months with money believers on the one side and Necker warning about a new Mississippi Bubble on the other. Common sense got lost as France got deeper and deeper into the fiscal mire. In April 1790, the first issue of 400 Million livres was released, backed by the church's property. This was the first Collateralized Debt Obligations (CDO's are derivatives, where banks package different types of debts together and sell them to investors. CDO's were

the derivative that was sold to investors and pension funds around the

World pre 2008. CDO's were rated as a high grade investment because a minor portion was good debt, while the underlying debt assets were mostly of «trash» value, as the underwriters knew the debt would not get repaid. They then bet against these investments and made massive profits on the fees they charged to investors. I will explain further in this chapter under the sub-title 2008 financial crisis.)

Months later the French Government had used up their money by deficit spending. Sounds familiar? The outcry for more money was getting louder and louder. The talks of issuing a second issue of new Assignates were on and after only 3 months it got approved by the assemble generale. In September 1790, a new issue of 800 million Assignates was approved. At this time gold, silver and copper currencies were starting to be hoarded by the people as yet again the elites failed to see past their greed. The government was still running a deficit. In August 1791, another 100 million Livre was issued. Everyone was blaming different things for the raising prices, but no one could figure out it was the increased money supply that was causing the prices to rise. At this point a speculative class emerged as one could start making money with money instead of doing more productive things like owning a business or being a farmer. They lobbied to issue more Assignates as it would automatically make them wealthier. These guys could be looked at as the traders on Wall Street today where the same thing is taking place as it did in the French economy since making money with money is always an endgame of Fiat currency.

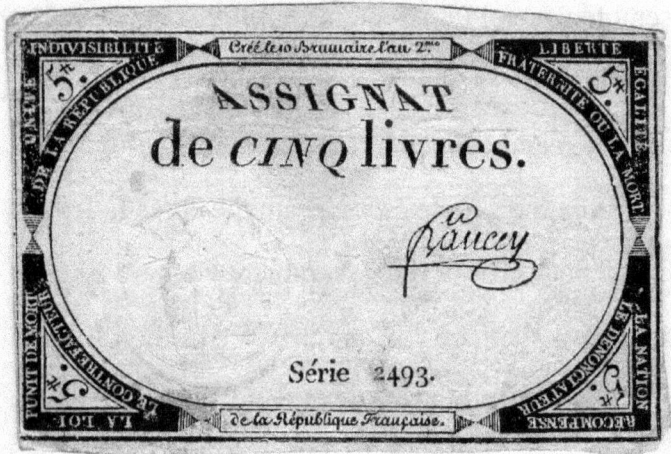

By December 1791, the first issue of livre had fallen almost 50% in value. In December, a new Finance minister who wanted more money printed got appointed and another issue of 800 million Assignate was issued. By the end of 1792, 3.5 billion Assignates had already been issued. Food price riots started. Since businessmen raised their prices astronomically, the government started putting in regulations and central planning. They put price caps on merchandise sold by the merchants. The outcome of this was that merchant's closed shop as they were forced to sell their merchandise under the free market value and received more and more worthless Assignates. The penalty for breaking government regulations was death and suddenly there were almost no merchants left. The government hunted them down and killed many as they went to sell on the black market instead. The printing presses heated up and by 1794 there were about 10 Billion Livre in circulation. In May 1795 another 10 B livre were printed up and in July 1795 another 14B livre were printed. Inflation was rampant and by October 1795 the death of the Assignate was a factum. A new currency called the Mandat was created, but it lasted just for a year as the loss of faith in Fiat Paper currency was manifest all over France. This was the end of an era in France and the French people were left poor and starving. Right after this, Napoleon's coup happened. Napoleon promised the people something that they believed in. This was the start of a vicious empire which conquered many countries. Napoleon pledged to the people that he would never instate a paper currency and the new Gold and Silver livre lasted all the way until World War 1.

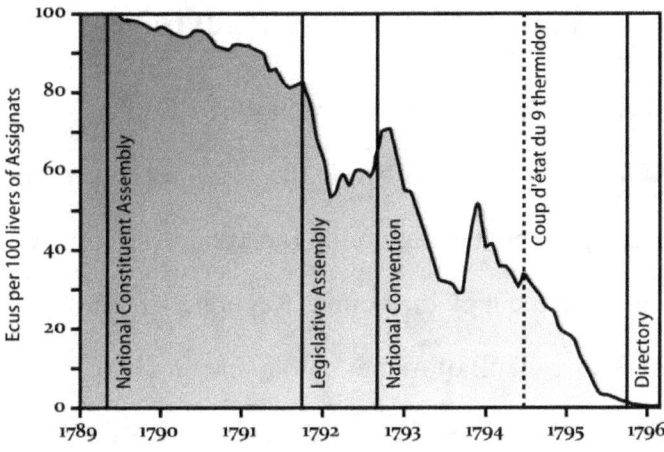

9

As you can see, yet again the people suffered greatly through oppression from the government, food shortages and starvation as they saw their lifelong wealth evaporate!

---

[9] Source Wikipedia

Weimar Republic (Germany)

I have met people from all around the world and a couple of them that have told me some amazing stories about currency devaluation in their countries. I have read about the lady in Weimar Republic who had a wheelbarrow full of money to buy bread. Her wheelbarrow was stolen and the money was left behind!

---

[10] Own Collection

Then there's the 5 Billion Reichmark bill which was so worthless that both its sides were not printed as the ink was more expensive than the face value of the 5 billion Reichmark. I've seen the pictures of kids playing with stacks of billion Reichmarks. And of people using the Fiat Currency to heat their house by burning it since it was cheaper than firewood.

---

[11] Own Collection

The hyperinflation episode in the Weimar Republic in the early 1920s was not the first, nor was it the very first one in Europe, or even the most extreme. Though probably it was the most famous instance of inflation in history (the Hungarian Pengo and Zimbabwean Dollar have both been even more inflated). However, as the most prominent case following the emergence of economics as a scholarly discipline, the Weimar hyperinflation drew interest in a way that previous instances had not. Many dramatic and unusual economic behaviours now associated with hyperinflation were first documented systematically in Germany: the order-of-magnitude increases in prices and interest rates, redenomination of the currency, consumer flight from cash to hard assets, and the rapid expansion of industries that produced those assets. German monetary economics was then highly influenced by Chartalism and the German Historical School, and this conditioned the way hyperinflation was then usually analysed.

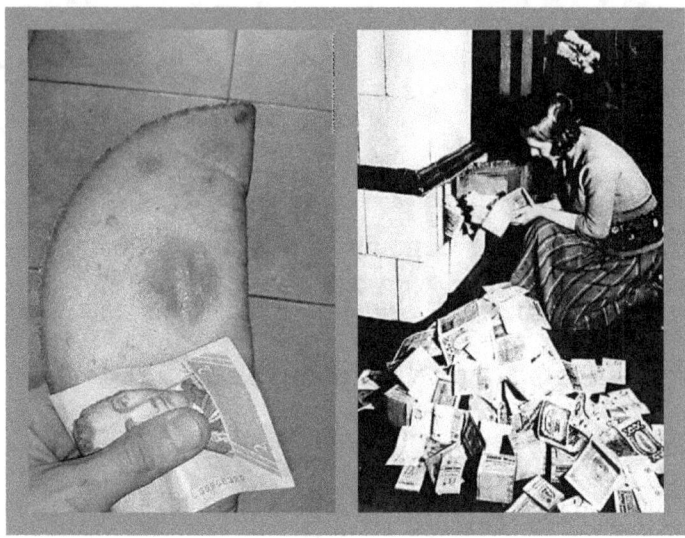

John Maynard Keynes described the situation in *The Economic Consequences of the Peace*: "The inflationism of the currency systems of Europe has proceeded to extraordinary lengths. The various belligerent Governments, unable, or too timid or too short-sighted to secure from loans or taxes the resources they required, have printed notes for the balance."

It was during this period of hyperinflation that French and British economic experts began to claim that Germany destroyed its economy with the purpose of avoiding reparations, but both these governments had conflicting views on how to handle the situation. The French declared that Germany should keep paying reparations, while Britain sought to grant a moratorium that would allow for its financial reconstruction.

Reparations accounted for about one third of the German deficit from 1920 to 1923, and were therefore cited by the German government as one of the main causes of hyperinflation. Other causes cited included bankers and speculators (particularly foreign). The inflation reached its peak by November 1923, but ended when a new currency (the Rentenmark) was introduced.

In order to make way for the new currency, banks "turned the marks over to junk dealers by the ton" to be recycled as paper.

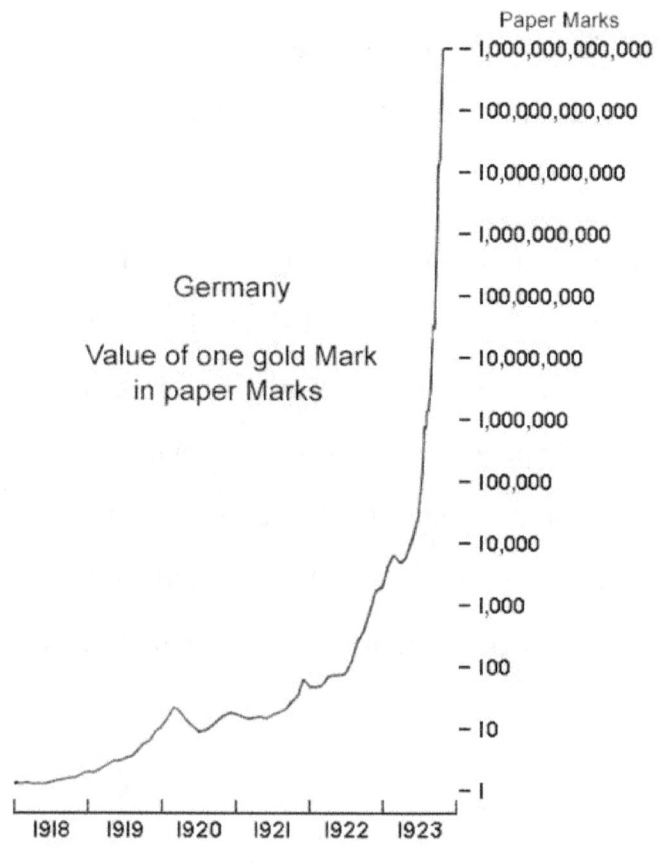

Bulgarian Leva Devaluation

Second Lev (1952–1962)

In 1952, following wartime inflation, a new lev replaced the original lev at a rate of 1 "new" lev = 100 "old" leva. However, the rate for banking accounts was different, ranging from 100:3 to 200:1. Prices for goods were replaced at a rate of 25:1. The new lev was pegged to the U.S. dollar at a rate of 6.8 leva = 1 dollar, falling to 9.52 leva on July 29, 1957.

Yugoslavia

In Yugoslavia during hyperinflation the Dinara price of goods doubled daily. In 1991 Yugoslavia erupted into civil war and the need for money to buy arms emerged. But the government had no taxation income as there was extremely high unemployment. The government chose to print money out of thin air and many people saw their lifelong savings demolished. The stores there had massive shortages due to sanctions against Yugolsavia along with businessmen going to black market sales in order to get hard currency over Deutche Mark.

The government started subsidizing food as they didn't want a revolution on their hands and then the people calmed down. Farmers sold their harvest to the government, but wanted either gold, silver or Deutche Mark over the Yugoslavian Dinar. By late 1993 and 1994, most goods were sold on the black market. Even the upper middle class struggled and as people made money they spent it right away. A system of checks were started, but most people didn't have money. This was almost a new currency running simultaneously. People receiving government pensions or social security lost the hardest as their pay checks didn't raise with the increase in inflation. At the maximum, inflation hit 313M% within a month. The Dinar failed miserably and people lost their wealth through the Fiat Currency System and Fractional Reserve Banking again! A new Dinar was created and it was pegged to the exchange rate of the Deutch Mark at the time.

1966–89; Hard Dinar

On January 1, 1966, the first of five revaluations took place, at a ratio of 100 to 1. This currency was never very stable, suffering from an inflation rate of 15 to 25 percent per year [1]. In the late 1980s the inflation rate accelerated, causing the currency to be revalued at the beginning of 1990.

1990–92; Convertible Dinar

The second revaluation took place on January 1, 1990, at a ratio of 10,000 to 1. During this period, the constituent republics began to leave the Socialist Federal Republic of Yugoslavia. Four out of six republics declared independence and issued their own currencies shortly after. This was the last Dinar that bore the coat of arms and the name of the "Socialist Federal Republic of Yugoslavia" in multiple languages.

Country	Currency	ISO code	Date Adopted	Value
Slovenia	Slovenian tolar	SIT	8 October 1991	1 dinar of 1990
Croatia	Croatian dinar	HRD	23 December 1991	1 dinar of 1990
Macedonia	Macedonian denar	MKD	26 April 1992	1 dinar of 1990
Bosnia and Herzegovina	Bosnian dinar	BAD	1 July 1992	1 dinar of 1992

Serbian enclaves in Croatia and Bosnia and Herzegovina also issued currencies in Dinar, equivalent to and revalued together with the Yugoslav Dinar. These were the Krajina Dinar and the Republika Srpska Dinar.

July 1992 – September 1993; Reformed Dinar

The third revaluation took place on 1 July 1992, at a ratio of 10 to 1. Hyperinflation began to occur during this currency's period of circulation. This dinar was issued in the then

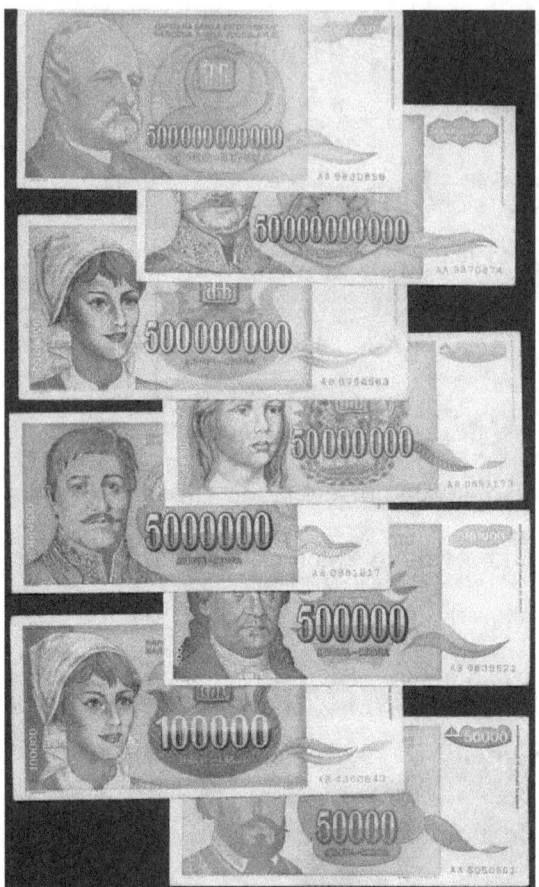

Federal Republic of Yugoslavia, which consisted of the remaining republics of Serbia and Montenegro. People started to use foreign hard currency, such as Deutsche Marks, to mitigate some of the problems of hyperinflation. (This federation split in 2006 and Montenegro currently uses the Euro as its currency, though it does not mint it.)

October–December 1993 Dinar

Yugoslavia re-denominated the Dinar for the fourth time on 1 October 1993, at a ratio of 1 million to 1. This did not mitigate hyperinflation, and the 1993 Dinar lasted for only three months.

Coinage became redundant. The 1993 Dinar had the largest denomination out of all incarnations of Yugoslavian currency: the banknote, featuring Jovan Jovanović Zmaj had a face value of 500 billion (5×10^{11}) dinara (right). Wages became worthless; if paid in cash, workers had to rush out and spend their wages before they lost their value overnight. Many businesses started to pay wages in goods instead, and a simple barter system developed. Businesses with good connections to politicians could still get access to hard currency.

Some shops, instead of rewriting their prices several times a day, started pricing goods in "bods" (points), often equivalent to hard currency such as one Deutschmark. The winter of 1993 was particularly hard for pensioners; if a monthly pension was spent immediately, it was still barely enough to buy three litres of milk. Many people relied on connections with friends and family abroad (who could provide hard currency) or in the countryside (who could grow food).

1994 dinar

Yugoslavia re-denominated the dinar for the fourth time on 1 January 1994, at a ratio of 1 billion (10^9) to 1.

The 1994 Dinar was the shortest-lived out of all incarnations of Yugoslavian currency, as hyperinflation continued to intensify, and only one coin (1 dinar) was issued for it. Towards the end of the 1994 Dinar, the National Bank overprinted and reissued 10 million Dinara banknotes from the 1992 Dinar (right).

Argentina

An Argentinian friend told me stories about 2 different defaults of the Argentinian Peso. In the mid 80's his dad had his account frozen where he had 57000 pesos. The next day the government devalued the currency 75%, which meant his dad's life savings were now only worth 25% of what they were earlier. If you had worked hard all of your life to retire comfortably and then the state takes 75% away from you, would you be angry? Would you believe in Fiat Currency?

My friend thought he was smart and had his money in his account in US Dollars. But he was in an Argentinian bank where they took his American dollars, exchanged them for Argentinian Peso, and then devalued the money 75%. So, he was still not safe.

Here is a documentary about the failure of the Argentine Peso and the 75% devaluation in 2001. This documentary is in Argentinian and texted in English.

Very important information that you should take the time to look at:

https://www.youtube.com/watch?v=Zsqa-YHE36A

Argentina has a reputation for not caring about printing currency. The once vibrant country got corrupted by the printing of the Peso and the constant devaluation of its currency through the 1900 to more current 2000s.

Here are some facts about Argentinian devaluation and how it caused many to flee the country. If you are caught in a country as a citizen you are the harvest that the government collects from through taxes.

The following table contains the monthly **historical exchange rates** of the different **currencies of Argentina**, expressed in Argentinian currency units per United States dollar, at the exchange rate **at the end of each month**.

From January 1914 to December 1969: pesos moneda nacional

From January 1970 to May 1983: pesos ley

From June 1983 to May 1985: peso argentino

	Jan	Feb	Mar	Apr	May	Jun	Jul	Aug	Sep	Oct	Nov	Dec
1914	2.3693	2.3750	2.3512	2.3602	2.3682	2.3682	2.3659					
1915	2.3636	2.3661	2.3795	2.3800	2.3815	2.3893	2.4055	2.4502	2.4489	2.4173	2.4143	2.3957
1916	2.3850	2.3732	2.3600	2.3614	2.3711	2.3743	2.4002	2.4152	2.3766	2.3361	2.3161	2.2761
1917	2.2893	2.2750	2.3014	2.3425	2.3095	2.2818	2.2959	2.3232	2.3325	2.2877	2.1918	2.1455
1918	2.2455	2.2855	2.2732	2.2475	2.2241	2.2377	2.2527	2.2564	2.2443	2.2364	2.2350	2.2223
1919	2.2323	2.2336	2.2527	2.2723	2.2611	2.3118	2.3516	2.3725	2.3616	2.3611	2.3305	2.3205
1920	2.3209	2.3155	2.3170	2.3295	2.3575	2.3830	2.4961	2.6407	2.7141	2.8145	2.9898	2.9282
1921	2.8966	2.8614	2.9327	3.1205	3.2268	3.3048	3.4541	3.4118	3.2589	3.1141	3.0866	3.0273

1922	2.9398	2.7550	2.7441	2.8157	2.7568	2.7730	2.7745	2.7668	2.8030	2.7870	2.7559	2.6525
1923	2.6805	2.6955	2.6984	2.7380	2.7845	2.8212	2.9273	3.0582	3.0348	3.0864	3.1986	3.1414
1924	3.0816	2.9684	2.9727	3.0439	3.0420	3.0722	3.0623	2.9577	2.8368	2.7177	2.6555	2.5682
1925	2.4934	2.5159	2.5361	2.6189	2.5168	2.4911	2.4770	2.4789	2.4766	2.4330	2.4061	2.4125
1926	2.4134	2.4395	2.5184	2.5023	2.4923	2.4805	2.4670	2.4734	2.4636	2.4509	2.4602	2.4355
1927	2.4225	2.3950	2.3650	2.3611	2.3614	2.3557	2.3539	2.3452	2.3407	2.3402	2.3441	2.3409
1928	2.3429	2.3418	2.3398	2.3418	2.3523	2.3491	2.3691	2.3743	2.3800	2.3793	2.3732	2.3768
1929	2.3750	2.3764	2.3809	2.3791	2.3834	2.3880	2.3841	2.3823	2.3839	2.3934	2.4207	2.4457
1930	2.4945	2.6386	2.6623	2.5745	2.6068	2.7016	2.7784	2.7614	2.7886	2.9218	2.9120	3.0216

1931	1932	1933	1934	1935	1936	1937	1938	1939
3.2655	3.8863	3.8863	3.2528	3.4735	3.4257	3.3058	3.4198	4.3661
3.1539	3.8863	3.8863	3.3117	3.4731	3.3994	3.3289	3.7606	4.3525
2.9089	3.8863	3.9191	3.3565	3.5375	3.4173	3.3303	3.9035	4.3435
2.9930	3.8863	3.7655	3.3227	3.4972	3.4359	3.2983	3.9026	4.3252
3.2232	3.8863	3.3614	3.4132	3.4702	3.4159	3.2950	3.8238	4.3209
3.2370	3.8863	3.2227	3.4444	3.4401	3.3872	3.2908	3.8395	4.3214
3.2609	3.8863	2.8443	3.4560	3.4306	3.3935	3.3121	3.8444	4.3235
3.5284	3.8863	2.8786	3.4080	3.4233	3.3888	3.3164	3.8759	4.3310
3.8155	3.8863	2.7555	3.4314	3.4488	3.3627	3.3389	3.9543	4.2779
4.2636	3.8863	2.6639	3.4517	3.4652	3.4587	3.3482	3.9823	4.2651
3.8975	3.8863	2.4973	3.4217	3.4530	3.4673	3.3782	4.2855	4.3127
3.8863	3.8863	3.2079	3.4527	3.4504	3.3098	3.4044	4.3964	4.3937

141

Year												
1940	4.3952	4.3042	4.2805	4.3514	4.4167	4.5497	4.6033	4.4400	4.3091	4.2654	4.2616	4.2423
1941	4.2335	4.2459	4.3283	4.2771	4.2209	4.2206	4.2129	4.2044	4.2314	4.2419	4.1956	4.2165
1942	4.2340	4.2382	4.2284	4.2262	4.2464	4.2561	4.2305	4.2175	4.2253	4.2174	4.2339	4.2401
1943	4.2421	4.2307	4.1963	4.0924	4.0009	3.9892	3.9904	3.9991	3.9997	3.9981	3.9966	3.9912
1944	3.9899	3.9940	4.0152	4.0181	4.0293	4.0277	4.0489	4.0424	4.0294	4.0330	4.0269	4.0407
1945	4.17	4.09	4.02	4.05	4.07	4.07	4.03	4.00	4.01	4.12	4.16	4.15
1946	4.22	4.19	4.19	4.17	4.12	4.09	4.13	4.10	4.14	4.13	4.17	4.21
1947	4.20	4.18	4.16	4.15	4.19	4.19	4.32	4.58	4.61	4.65	4.49	4.48
1948	4.51	4.44	4.44	4.59	5.10	5.63	6.01	6.54	7.16	8.87	8.53	8.50

1949	9.84	9.06	9.06	9.56	10.01	9.56	9.36	9.81	11.88	13.02	15.21	15.86
1950	15.20	14.80	13.90	13.75	13.95	13.74	15.50	17.25	18.05	19.65	19.55	16.50
1951	16.85	15.50	18.20	19.50	25.50	24.10	24.50	28.60	29.50	27.90	27.75	27.00
1952	28.60	26.50	24.50	25.00	23.10	21.25	21.50	20.40	19.80	20.50	21.00	23.15
1953	23.25	22.75	22.85	23.75	23.80	23.60	23.85	21.95	22.75	22.25	19.80	20.10
1954	22.25	22.60	23.25	25.00	26.00	25.50	26.15	26.25	26.50	26.50	26.95	26.70
1955	27.85	28.10	28.40	29.50	31.85	33.25	30.75	31.50	27.00	29.15	32.50	36.00
1956	40.50	42.85	40.50	37.80	35.20	32.60	30.20	32.50	30.80	32.10	34.90	36.55
1957	37.40	36.70	40.50	37.00	40.25	40.75	42.50	43.85	43.00	39.25	37.00	37.20

Year												
1958	37.25	38.25	40.50	42.00	42.30	42.10	42.50	46.50	54.25	73.50	71.50	70.50
1959	65.30	68.70	68.40	80.80	88.80	84.90	86.00	83.50	82.50	82.30	83.10	83.30
1960	82.90	82.70	82.90	83.40	82.80	82.50	82.60	82.60	83.00	82.70	82.85	82.65
1961	82.75	82.60	82.90	83.50	82.80	82.60	82.75	83.50	83.25	83.45	83.30	84.20
1962	83.55	83.40	83.80	99.50	112.50	133.00	118.40	126.30	128.80	139.60	148.40	134.10
1963	134.40	135.20	140.30	137.20	138.80	139.00	134.00	134.60	149.60	146.80	140.80	132.50
1964	134.25	130.90	138.25	142.70	140.40	156.55	174.15	169.35	161.22	166.05	179.41	192.89
1965	215.00	223.38	217.88	227.00	248.00	276.20	285.71	272.34	258.18	233.07	225.00	233.90
1966	247.37	238.16	228.88	222.78	234.90	238.29	224.65	227.98	247.35	256.18	266.78	270.60

1967	1968	1969	1970	1971	1972	1973	1974	1975
282.22	350.00	350.00	**3.4975**	4.2750	10.15	12.13	11.90	22.65
295.77	350.00	349.75	3.5000	4.1750	10.35	11.45	12.30	23.45
345.24	349.75	349.50	3.4850	4.3350	10.00	11.43	12.40	28.35
348.18	349.50	350.25	3.4950	4.6350	10.15	12.50	13.30	36.45
348.75	350.00	351.75	3.5125	4.8050	11.95	12.50	14.40	47.00
349.25	349.50	352.00	4.0100	5.2550	11.75	10.88	14.90	53.00
350.00	349.50	351.25	4.0100	5.3750	11.20	10.10	16.60	66.50
349.75	350.00	351.75	4.0075	5.8050	13.00	10.95	17.55	76.00
349.75	350.00	351.75	4.0175	6.9050	13.70	11.10	18.70	110.00
349.50	350.00	351.50	4.1650	8.8500	12.00	10.60	20.05	142.50
349.50	350.00	351.50	4.2900	9.7750	11.88	10.58	20.90	132.50
350.00	350.00	**352.25**	4.3350	9.4000	11.25	11.20	22.00	127.50

1976	1977	1978	1979	1980	1981	1982	1983	1984
196.00	297.50	636.50	1,048.50	1,659.50	2,038.50	10,300	69,250	35.25
270.00	332.50	679.50	1,098.50	1,698.50	2,267.50	10,000	80,000	44.85
325.00	342.50	717.50	1,151.50	1,745.50	**2,485.50**	11,850	93,250	52.85
255.00	364.50	759.50	1,202.50	1,782.50	**3,200**	14,800	93,500	58.40
245.00	372.50	765.50	1,257.50	1,819.50	3,625	21,250	**98,500**	65.65
247.50	390.00	783.50	1,310.50	1,854.50	7,050	24,250	**11.50**	73.65
250.00	411.50	797.50	1,365.50	1,872.50	7,200	58,500	14.75	82.25
263.00	437.50	832.50	1,414.50	1,910.50	7,300	49,000	19.30	108.50
247.00	468.50	861.50	1,463.50	1,932.50	7,590	47,500	25.90	121.80
245.50	510.50	911.50	1,515.50	1,946.50	9,050	55,000	24.10	139.25
273.00	550.50	956.50	1,567.50	1,972.50	11,100	63,500	24.15	180.50
276.00	599.50	998.00	1,611.50	1,997.50	10,400	68,000	25.65	205.00

1985	1986	1987	1988	1989	1990	1991	1992	1993
266.00	0.885	1.613	5.50	17.72	1,870	9,250	**0.9905**	0.9991
356.00	0.865	1.720	6.18	28.20	5,750	10,275	0.9899	0.9991
464.00	0.925	2.035	6.48	47.90	4,675	9,630	0.9934	0.9997
557.50	0.910	2.070	7.35	79.00	4,925	9,833	0.9895	0.9978
673.00	0.890	2.060	9.21	290	5,005	9,923	0.9895	1.0001
0.855	0.880	2.145	11.32	540	5,310	9,993	0.9915	0.9983
0.950	0.925	2.553	12.65	665	5,465	9,973	0.9919	0.9996
0.950	1.165	3.083	14.40	665	6,305	9,973	0.9910	1.0013
0.900	1.213	3.625	14.96	650	5,730	9,903	0.9911	1.0013
0.930	1.265	4.045	15.08	723	5,570	9,913	0.9911	0.9991
0.865	1.425	4.36	15.60	1,020	5,170	9,909	0.9928	0.9975
0.875	1.668	5.10	16.41	1,950	5,820	**10,028**	0.9916	0.9984

1994	0.9984	1.0015	1.0011	0.9986	0.9985	0.9974	0.9984	0.9991	0.9993	0.9990	0.9999	1.0014
1995	1.0006	1.0017	1.0009	1.0011	0.9986	0.9989	0.9994	0.9984	0.9989	1.0003	0.9992	1.0016
1996	0.9992	0.9998	0.9997	0.9995	1.0000	1.0006	1.0012	1.0001	1.0002	0.9995	0.9989	1.0005
1997	0.9985	0.9993	0.9994	0.9995	0.9993	1.0005	0.9998	0.9996	0.9995	1.0022	1.0007	1.0014
1998	0.9988	0.9989	1.0007	1.0001	0.9997	0.9997	1.0002	1.0019	1.0001	1.0035	0.9999	1.0010
1999	1.0003	0.9999	0.9987	0.9994	1.0014	1.0049	0.9997	1.0004	0.9990	1.0000	1.0070	1.0014
2000	0.9996	0.9987	0.9991	0.9987	1.0009	0.9984	0.9990	0.9986	0.9989	0.9999	1.0004	1.0014
2001	0.9992	0.9996	1.0009	1.0001	0.9994	1.0010	1.0290	0.9974	0.9989	1.0029	1.0038	**1.1499**
2002	**1.9500**	**2.0000**	**2.9500**	**2.9750**	**3.6000**	**3.8500**	3.6900	3.6100	3.7400	3.5150	3.6200	3.4050

2003	2004	2005	2006	2007	2008	2009	2010	2011
3.2050	2.9750	2.9240	3.0660	3.1070	3.1580	3.4880	3.8350	4.0080
3.2050	2.9150	2.9380	3.0740	3.1000	3.1610	3.5670	3.8590	4.0300
2.9750	2.8650	2.9170	3.0820	3.1000	3.1680	3.7200	3.8780	4.0540
2.8250	2.8450	2.9100	3.0480	3.0900	3.1640	3.7140	3.8880	4.0800
2.8550	2.9600	2.8830	3.0850	3.0770	3.0990	3.7490	3.9290	4.0900
2.8000	2.9550	2.8870	3.0860	3.0930	3.0250	3.7970	3.9310	4.1100
2.9150	2.9750	2.8610	3.0720	3.1210	3.0440	3.8300	3.9400	4.1450
2.9450	3.1050	2.9110	3.0970	3.1560	3.0300	3.8510	3.9500	4.2000
2.9050	2.9850	2.9100	3.1040	3.1500	3.1350	3.8430	3.9600	4.2050
2.8500	2.9750	3.0020	3.0890	3.1420	3.3880	3.8190	3.9570	4.2360
2.9700	2.9450	2.9660	3.0680	3.1450	3.3730	3.8110	3.9880	4.2810
2.9400	2.9750	3.0320	3.0620	3.1490	3.4530	3.8000	3.9760	4.3040

2012	4.3370	4.3570	4.3790	4.4170	4.4710	4.5270	4.5850	4.6380	4.6970	4.7660	4.7830	4.9200
2013	4.9480	5.0090	5.0870	5.1530	5.2360	5.3300	5.4400	5.5810	5.7370	5.8480	6.0120	6.3380
2014	7.0720	7.8490	7.9290	8.0020	8.0390	8.1250	8.1600	8.3170	8.4190	8.4790	8.5140	8.5510
2015	8.6000	8.6840	8.7700									

From June 1985 to December 1991: australes

From January 1992: pesos

The value of one current peso is 10,000,000,000,000 (trillion) *pesos moneda nacional* (m$n), the currency in use from 1881 to 1969. It is also equal, as of March 2015, to more than 37,000,000,000,000 (trillion) 1914 pesos with the U.S. dollar as reference – an average annual depreciation relative to the dollar of 27%. The Argentinians have survived about 5-6 devaluations and most times the only way they survived was that the people who kept their wealth in commodities were the few who won. You need to understand that if you use a commodity and not Fiat Currency, you will have something that will never lose its value as it would be useful either as food or to make things with.

Zimbabwe

The hyperinflation of Zimbabwe's currency, the Zimbabwean Dollar, is historically the worst inflation to ever destroy a currency. What happened in Zimbabwe was a new way of a currency's destruction. It was destroyed by greed and co-option as Zimbabwean elites found they could buy the land, but that destroyed their country as no other country was willing to do business with them in their currency. Just think - suppose you went to a store. By the time you left to check out your loot you found that it had raised twice in price as you were shopping. This was a daily happening in Zimbabwe in 2007-2008. If you had $100k in Zimbabwean dollars in 2001, you could in early 2001 use your saved-up money to buy just a grain of salt. Maybe not literally, but this statement is pretty close to the reality of living in Zimbabwe. Yet again, saving money in Fiat Currency would make you a loser! School tuition changed 1 times a week in 2006 to about 2 times a day 2008. It was almost impossible to have exchange rates to other currencies as people used the free market to make decisions at any moment. You went to the store to buy bread. First of all, $2B gave you only one loaf. Then when you went to pay for it, it was already up at a price of $3-4B at check out. Although the raising prices gave the chance for stores to claim higher costs of their merchandise, this was only the beginning! In early 2008, they started printing the $100T bill.

Here is an example of what happened with inflation as a destructive force. It cost $200T to buy a 24 pack of beer and only 3 weeks later, the same $200T bought you just one beer. That is about 2400% inflation. Or a 95.5% depreciation of your asset.

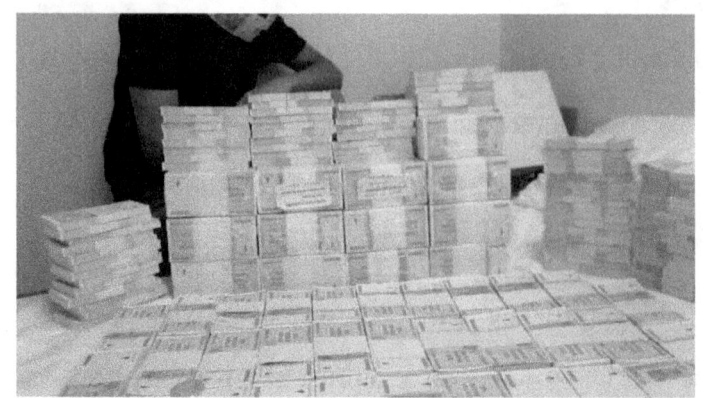

When the inflation started to get really rampant, smart business people found a new way of counting the money. They were not bankers, but they still had to use note counters in order to count money fast enough to not get big waiting lines to pay. Note counters was only the start. After a while the currency became so worthless that they started to do what had been done in the Weimar Republic - counting money by weight or bundles of 1000 bills of one denomination. At this time, there were millions of millionaires, billionaires and trillionairs. Think about today - how we get more and more millionaires and billionaires. That is not to say there is an increase of wealth of the richest. Due to the increase in money supply the wealthiest families' assets have risen in value, and an increase in true wealth is only an illusion. This is not to say that they do not use this to their advantage, as they use their easy access to cheap money to buy more assets and automatically the asset will increase in value.

Instead of wallets, bags, briefcases and wheelbarrows were used to move money around. Using other currencies was prohibited and many times if a person was found possessing them, they were charged and given prison time. At that time, Zimbabwe's main industry was the mining sector with gold, silver, copper, coal and diamonds being the main commodities being mined. There were quite high trade commodities to cash, but it was illegal. If someone was caught mining without the government licenses, they had to serve up to 4 years in prison. Commodities started to win over paper money as more and more people started to understand how commodities retained their value and wealth. Accordingly, the use and accumulation of these commodities started to ramp up. At one point it became illegal to possess any foreign currency. Fuel started to become a currency as fuel, like gasoline, is very important for our survival. People understood that carrying around cans of fuel would be very inconvenient and so a coupon currency backed by fuel was adopted as a simultaneous currency along with the Zimbabwe currency.

As trade slowed, Zimbabwean Central Bankers printed currency like crazy but with absolutely no result. The only result was a massive increase in inflation. Does that sound like what is slowly happening around the world today? Police corruption increased as police were more willing to get commodities like alcohol instead for Zimbabwean Dollars as fines. The downward spiral had started and the power outages and other infrastructure deteriorated as tools or commodities needed to run utilities could not be imported since no one wanted the failing currency.

The Zimbabwean dollar was replaced by the US dollar in 2009.

Date	Rate	Date	Rate	Date	Rate	Date	Rate	Date	Rate
1980	7%	1981	14%	1982	15%	1983	19%	1984	10%
1985	10%	1986	15%	1987	10%	1988	7.3%	1989	14%
1990	17%	1991	48%	1992	40%	1993	20%	1994	25%
1995	28%	1996	16%	1997	20%	1998	48%	1999	56.9%
2000	55.22%	2001	112.1%	2002	198.93%	2003	598.75%	2004	132.75%
2005	585.84%	2006	1,281.11%	2007	66,212.3%	2008 Jul.	231,150,888.	2008 Aug.	471,000,000,

Date	Rate
2008 Sep.	3,840,000,000,000,000,0%
2008 Mid-Nov.	89,700,000,000,000,000,000,000%

The 2008 Crisis

Massive fraud was involved in the worst economic crisis in history as the debt load in US and many western countries had reached its limits.

---

[12] Own Collection

What brought Fiat currency and Fractional Reserve Banking system to its knees in 2008 was a new financial engineering tool called derivatives. In 2006, Lawrence Summers was caught saying derivatives would make the world securer. Well, he was completely wrong!

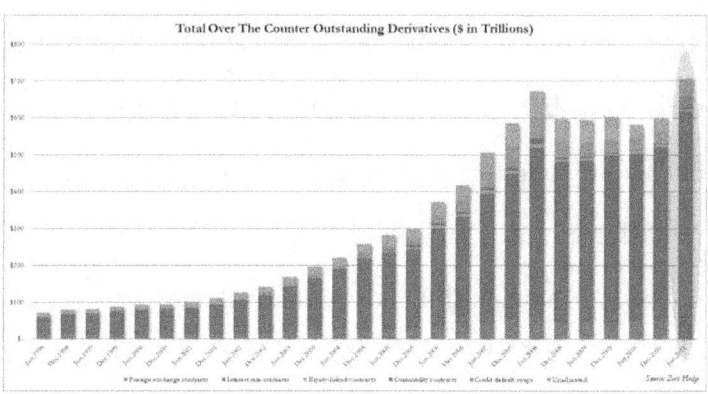

Here is what the bankers did! They had over lent money to people in the mortgage market. They got greedy and started to fake mortgage applications so they looked real. These mortgages were called NINJA loans (No Income No Job and Assets). These loans were given to people who could not pay them back as they had no money. The bubble should have popped before this but in a last attempt they chose to start defrauding and luring people into houses they could not afford. It is as bad as a mortgage since the bank owns your house till the last dollar is paid.

You would think - how could a couple of billions in loans bring down a global economy? The answer is complicated, but easy to understand! The bankers didn't stop at fraudulent loans! They took these loans to rating agencies which are supposed to rate an asset. They paid them off to get AAA ratings which meant the it was the best possible asset. Then they took these assets and put them into a package with other debts which were high-end loans, but as these loans started failing the promised ROI deteriorated and went negative. On top of this, these assets called CDOs (Collateralized Debt Obligations) were not sold once but twice, thrice and even four times to banks, pension funds, and hedge funds worldwide. Then, to make the fraud come a full circle, banks like Merril Lynch, Goldman Sachs and Bank of America, together with JP Morgan, took these debt derivative tools and insured them at AIG, one of the world's biggest insurance corporations. And it didn't stop there. In the end they started betting against the investments that they had created and sold on a platform created by AIG.

In other words, the banks won and the people lost. The banks that failed were mostly bailed out with tax payers' money though the TARP program (Troubled Asset Relief Program) which gave $700B to banks in what is called corporate welfare or socialism. We were stolen from!

What you need to understand is that crises like these are merely a sign of economic structural distress as our system is failing and the crises of 1980s, 2001 and 2008 will become even more rampant as debts need to increase at an ever high pace to keep up with the demand to pay the interest accrued and people need to work harder and harder.

The need for higher taxes and ever longer workdays will enslave us totally to the bankers. If you paid off all the debt in the world, there would basically be no money left except M0 which is reserves created by central banks, but the reserves cannot pay the remaining interest owed to the bankers or is it enough value created to keep the system going? The question is, does the accumulated debt secured to an asset? Meaning having an asset backing debt against housing or a business is innovative and creates something of value to society. Most debt today is unsecured debt, which is margin debt on investments. Personal debt and overextended credit card debt is typically finances all the meaningless stuff in our lives. This stuff has no value and when accumulated you suddenly sit with no cash flow at the end of the month. Which means we will default on our loans and "legally" the bankers can claim your asset to be theirs since you could not pay the remaining money owed on that asset, whether is a house, car, an investment that went sour, a business loan or another loan the bank might have given you. The remnant of 2008 is a total collapse of a real productive and innovative economy. We have become obsolete, as bankers continue to practice what the bankers did during the French revolution - **they do not need people working anymore to make money**. Making money with money is the only way for us to survive in this debt ridden society. We are left to pay the accrued interest as the only means of preventing a full systemic collapse, as the debt mountain is unsustainable and unsecured. The bankers are always the winners in any scenario. The current initiative of the economic world is not to increase interest rates. The Central Bank has set the lowest interest rates in world history. Together with an ever increasing debt around the world the Ponzi scheme needs growth in debt in order to pay the ever increasing charge of interest, which does not have any real commodity asset attached to it. This Ponzi scheme creates zero value for the economy while destroying citizen's personal savings which they acquired through hard work, innovation and value creation. What we are learning is that today's system is only in place to steal wealth from people by luring them into debt and using a fiat currency that can be printed as and when the governments feel like it. As you can see the Arab Spring is merely an extension of the death of money around the world as corruption has become rampant by the creation of currency. Growing frustration about prices of food and other commodities fueled a prairie fire through the desert areas of the Arab countries.

Business people were fed up with the laws enforced upon them with absolutely no freedom

Governments usually print a lot of money to buy weapons either to destroy or control each other. What I see as an end game is a massive printing of money as deflation will destroy the Ponzi system. The only way out of total destruction of a currency is educating people well before a revolution happens!

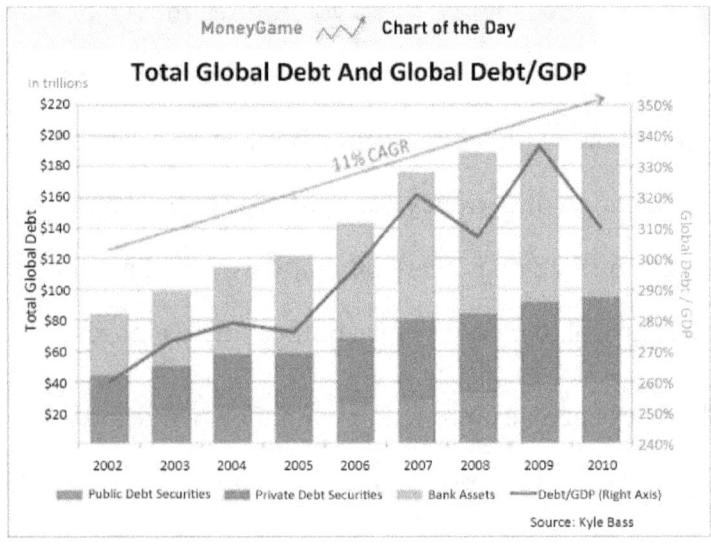

[13]

---

[13] Source Kyle Bass

The Arab Spring

The failure of understanding the true causes of the Arab Spring has been costly for many Arab countries. Yes, the people are fed up with tyrannical governments, but the underlying monetary causes is the real cause of the Arab Spring!

Here are some stats:

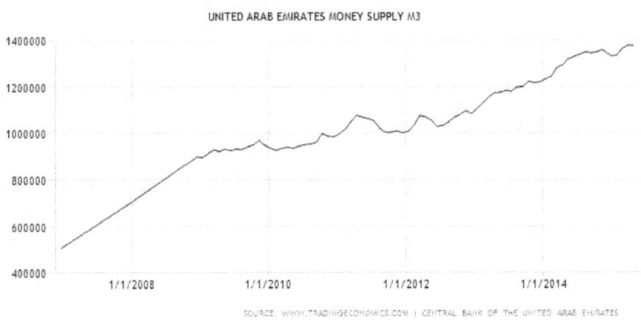

14

---

[14] Source http://www.tradingeconomics.com Publicly available numbers

15

16

---

[15] Source http://www.tradingeconomics.com Publicly available numbers

[16] Source http://www.tradingeconomics.com Publicly available numbers

---

[17] Source http://www.tradingeconomics.com Publicly available numbers

[18] Source http://www.tradingeconomics.com Publicly available numbers

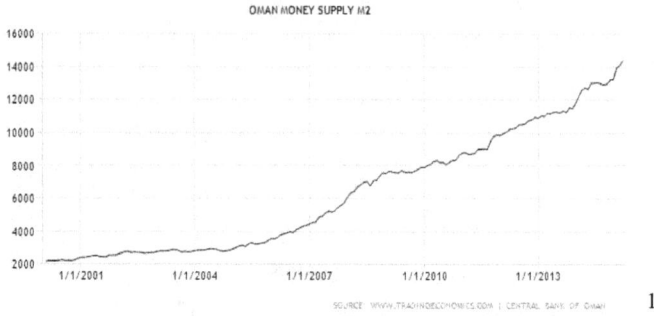

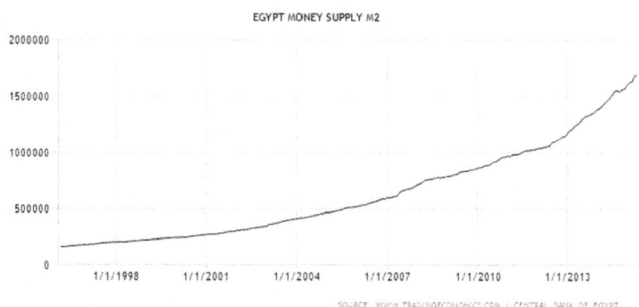

---

[19] Source http://www.tradingeconomics.com Publicly available numbers

[20] Source http://www.tradingeconomics.com Publicly available numbers

[21]

[21] Source http://www.tradingeconomics.com Publicly available numbers

[22] Source http://www.tradingeconomics.com Publicly available numbers

[23]

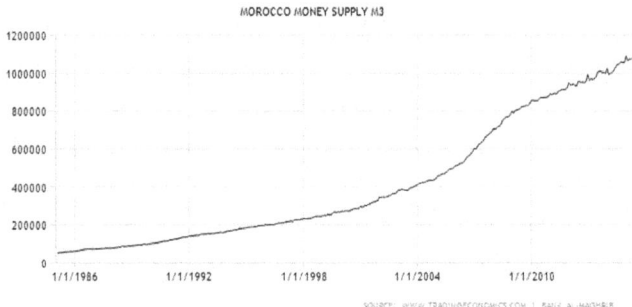

[24]

---

[23] Source http://www.tradingeconomics.com Publicly available numbers

[24] Source http://www.tradingeconomics.com Publicly available numbers

Current economic turmoil and war in Ukraine

Ukraine is getting destroyed by civil war. War is usually caused by the system or when the system is used to dominate others. Printing of currency is often used to buy weapons in order to build up for war or conquering. Here is how the war and printing of the Ukrainian Hryvnia is destroying the Ukrainian population's wealth

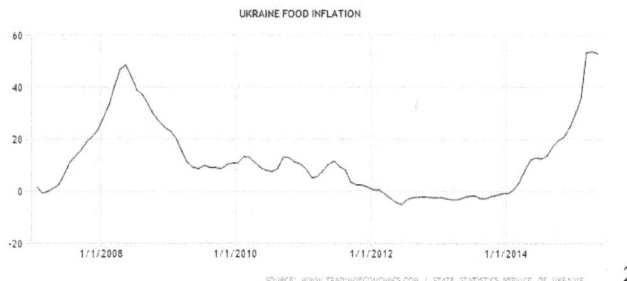

[26]

---

[26] Source http://www.tradingeconomics.com Publicly available numbers

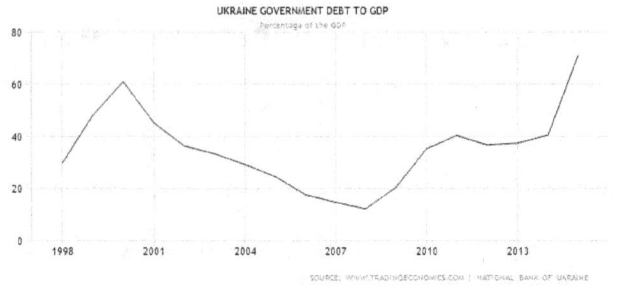

27

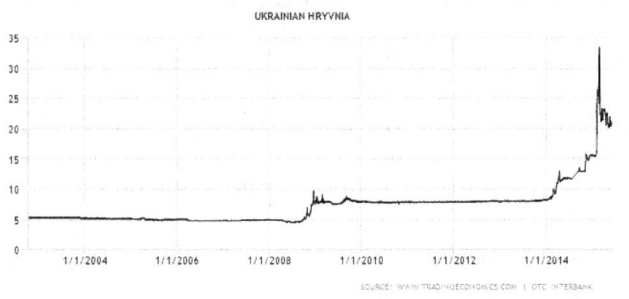

28

---

[27] Source http://www.tradingeconomics.com Publicly available numbers

[28] Source http://www.tradingeconomics.com Publicly available numbers

[29]

[30]

---

[29] Source http://www.tradingeconomics.com Publicly available numbers

[30] Source http://www.tradingeconomics.com Publicly available numbers

[31]

A quick story from Ukraine

Valentyna is thankful for the two pensions her and her husband share, even if Ukraine's inflation shock means they're no longer enough to buy medicine and meat.

---

[31] Source http://www.tradingeconomics.com Publicly available numbers

As you can see the Arab Spring is merely an extension of the death of money around the world as corruption has become rampant by the creation of currency. Growing frustration about prices of food and other commodities fuelled a prairie fire through the desert areas of the Arab countries.

Business people were fed up with the laws enforced upon them with absolutely no freedom and officials taking advantage of them everyday by stealing outright from them. The fuel for the fire that started it all was literally human flesh as a frustrated businessman from Tunisia ended up setting himself on fire in frustration. The guy who started the Arab spring died before he got to see what he started.

As you also can see in the charts above is that the purchasing power of many Arab countries depreciated fast.

As you can see the Arab Spring is merely an extension of the death of money around the world as corruption has become rampant by the creation of currency. Growing frustration about prices of food and other commodities fuelled a prairie fire through the desert areas of the Arab countries.

Business people were fed up with the laws enforced upon them with absolutely no freedom fast

Here are some facts about the Arab spring:

By January 2015, rulers had been forced from power in Tunisia, Egypt (twice), Libya, and Yemen (twice); civil uprisings had erupted in Bahrain and Syria; major protests had broken out in Algeria, Iraq, Jordan, Kuwait, Morocco, Israel and Sudan; and minor protests had occurred in Mauritania, Oman, Saudi Arabia, Djibouti, Western Sahara, and Palestine. Weapons and Tuareg fighters returning from the Libyan Civil War stoked a simmering conflict in Mali which has been described as "fallout" from the Arab Spring in North Africa.

Some of the causes supposed to have spawned the uprising are Authoritarianism, Demographics, Political Corruptions, Inflation, Imperialism, Kleptocracy (big corporations taking advantages of people and stealing money in collusion with governments), Sectarianism, Unemployment, the burning of himself by Tunisian businessman Mohamed Bouazizi and supposed higher food prices caused by Russian export ban as many crops were damaged in a wild fire.

Although there are many causes behind the uprising, there are also several factors that were caused due to a failed monetary system which killed thousands and created chaos.

The problem with a revolution is that you need to educate yourself on what you want as the loss of your wealth and purchasing power makes you desperate and you are then willing to vote for anyone who promises something better than what you currently have. Similar to the Weimar Republic failure, many Arab spring countries were now worse off as tyrannies were replaced with more tyranny and destruction of infrastructure.

As mentioned earlier and seen from the outcome of the Weimar Republic and the Reichmarks failure, nothing good ever comes out of listening to leaders promising you things for free or witnessing the destruction of someone else's livelihood who is a scapegoat of currency failure! The only people to blame are the elite who are in control of the currency, both its creation and its supply!

"We have some potatoes, tomatoes and cucumbers from our dacha," said the 72-year-old pensioner as she made her way through the city of Zhytomyr, a two-hour bus ride west of Kiev. "I can't imagine how people survive on a single pension. We can't even go to the drug store. We try to use herbs instead."

From Lviv, near the Polish border, to Kharkiv, 1,000 kilometres (650 miles) east in Russia's shadow, Ukrainians are grappling with the world's worst-performing currency, inflation that's rocketed to 20 percent and the worst recession in five years. The plight of Zhytomyr's 270,000 residents shows how bailout-mandated austerity and the strains of an eight-month insurgency are playing out in everyday life.

Standoff in Ukraine

Across the street from the city's Soviet-era department store, the central open-air market sells food, clothes and toys. Traders huddle next to signs offering pumpkin seeds, nuts, rabbit pelts, feathers and beans from producers who've travelled from nearby villages.

Locals are cutting back because of this year's 48 percent plunge in the Hryvnia, a decline that's eroded purchasing power. The inflation rate spiked to 19.8 percent last month as the currency's slide boosted the costs of imported goods from gasoline to fruit.

'Cheapest Soap'

"I feel the hryvnia devaluation everywhere," Tamara Yakovets, 46, said from the window of her 2-square-meter kiosk, where she sells toothpaste and shampoo. "My clients are shocked. I have to raise prices every week. People stopped buying expensive stuff and now they ask for the cheapest soap."

Inflation will probably speed up to 25 percent this year, compared with the 19 percent forecast earlier, central bank Governor Valeriya Gontareva said today.

Ukrainians are no strangers to inflation. Price growth peaked at 10,256 percent in 1993 as the Soviet economy was dismantled. Having subsided, the rate jumped to 31.3 percent in 2008, shortly before the hryvnia sank last.

The focus is on the currency again. Aside from imports, expenses from renting an apartment to buying a car are frequently fixed in dollars, while salaries are in hryvnia.

For Iryna Ivanchuk, even a wage in hryvnia would be a relief. Since losing her job this year, she's gotten by on her husband's military stipend and assistance from relatives.

Dollar Watch

"I watch the dollar rate all the time because for me it's the best indicator of poverty," said the 29-year-old mother of a son in first grade. "I buy less sweets and fruit because of the astronomical costs. We used to save some money. Now, we can't save anything."

Ukraine's hryvnia rebounded to 15.18 per dollar as of 1:23 p.m. in Kiev, data compiled by Bloomberg show. It's gained about 4 percent since Nov. 11

Adding to the burden, the government is raising the price of natural gas to meet the terms of a $17 billion international bailout. While that will stem the drain on state funds from subsidies, it's putting pressure on households as heating and power costs jump.

The cabinet, battling an economic contraction that the central bank estimates will reach 7.5 percent this year, must address declining living standards, according to Alexander Valchyshen, chief economist at Investment Capital Ukraine in Kiev. Spiralling prices are as much of a threat to order as the conflict in the eastern Donbas region, he said.

'Proper Policies'

"Inflation is the same as the war," Valchyshen said. "It may lead to protests if people blame the authorities for failing to conduct proper policies."

The government has promised to help the poor pay their utility bills and is expanding a program to boost the number of households covered to 4 million from 1 million. The World Bank approved a $300 million loan in July to help Ukraine widen assistance to the vulnerable and socially excluded.

Some Ukrainians are prepared to stomach the economic pain as a cost of leaving Russia's orbit and aligning with the European Union. President Petro Poroshenko has signed a political association and trade pact with the 28-member bloc, a key demand of the protesters who toppled his predecessor in February.

Not Infinite

"I'm ready to tolerate the current economic situation as long as the war is on," said Hanna Hryhoriyeva, 67, a teacher at a culinary college who backed the protests' anti-corruption message. "I won't go onto the streets tomorrow because of inflation and the devaluation but my patience isn't infinite."

Others are less understanding.

Valya, a pensioner who declined to give her last name, said she'd just bought 2 kilograms (4.4 pounds) of grain that should last a month, along with potatoes and beetroot from the market. While she doesn't drink alcohol or smoke, she can't afford the bus to visit relatives' graves in the Lviv region.

"Glory to Ukraine?" said Valya, 76, referring to a slogan of the street uprising. "Glory for what? Higher prices? The war? We're just tolerating the authorities."

Ending the war, where a two-month truce hasn't stopped the fatalities, is key for Valentyna, who's already living without medicine and meat. With pensions flat as prices increase, everyone is feeling the pain that's forced her to cut back.

"This is how we survive," Valentyna said, declining to give her last name. "The main thing we need is peace."

Current Venezuela inflation caused by low oil price

Venezuela has a centrally planned economy. This is the opposite of a Free Market Economy where the people decide the prices of goods and the interest on money when borrowed from someone. A collectivist economy is never a good idea. Venezuela's current economic turmoil with its rapid debt accumulation, high interest rates and shortages is apparent. Oil prices have declined lately and this has caused huge issues for the Venezuelan government as they are dependent on oil as an income towards their budget.

The recent dip in the oil prices has forced Venezuela into printing money to keep their economy afloat.

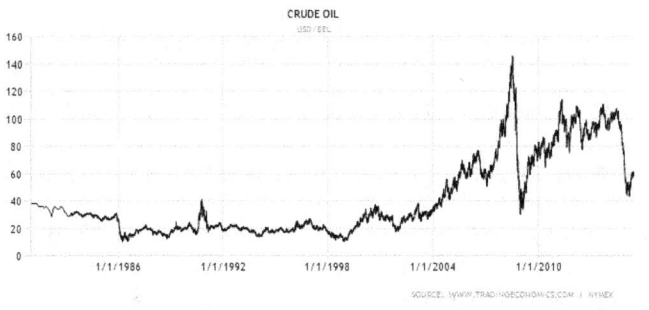

32

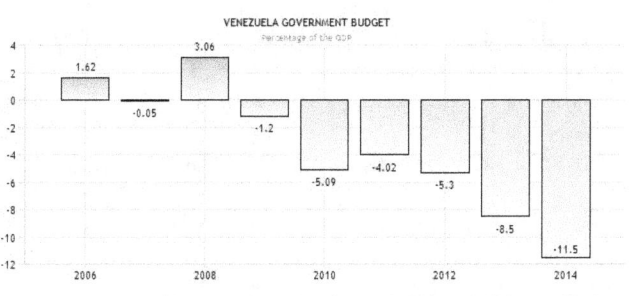

33

---

[32]Source http://www.tradingeconomics.com Publicly available numbers

[33]Source http://www.tradingeconomics.com Publicly available numbers

You can see from these charts a clear pattern emerging, which shows becoming dependent on income from a commodity to spend money on socialist economy's welfare programs. With raising inflation the money is simply not there to afford the welfare system. Shortages in supply have already started to appear as the Venezuelan Bolivar gets less and less popular since it is rapidly losing its value. Throughout the year, many times there have even been several toilet paper shortages.

Recently, as inflation is becoming more rampant in food and other merchandise the shortages have increased as the government has lost control of their central planning. Instead of buying food for their citizens, they pay the debts that they have racked up. In fact, it is not even debt, rather it is just the interest as no countries pay their debts anymore

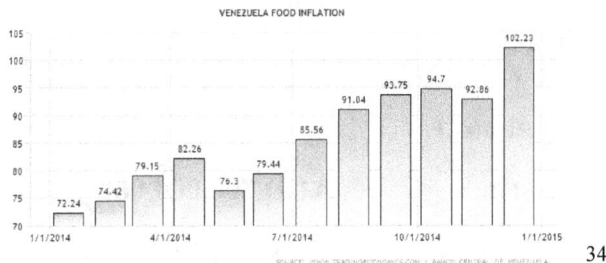

[34]

This death cycle of debt Venezuela entered will cause its demise.

High Yields is like a bottle of wine let open outside for wasps to swarm.

As we live in a financialized world the bankers were the wasps chasing high yields, and bought Venezuelan Government bond and corporate debt. The cash-strapped Venezuelan government had a choice to make. Either pay their investors or have money for food. They paid their investors.

Here is an overview of Venezuelan Outstanding debt.

---

[34] Source http://www.tradingeconomics.com Publicly available numbers

Outstanding bond issues

SECTOR: CORPORATE

2 issues outstanding worth **AUD 500 000 000**

8 issues outstanding worth **CHF 2 105 000 000**

1 issue outstanding worth **CNY 600 000 000**

2 issues outstanding worth **EUR 1 400 000 000**

2 issues outstanding worth **JPY 14 600 000 000**

1 issue outstanding worth **NOK 1 500 000 000**

22 issues outstanding worth **USD 40 642 302 800**

15 issues outstanding worth **VEB 123 144 268 251**

SECTOR: SOVEREIGN

24 issues outstanding worth **USD 37 217 908 559**

23 issues outstanding worth **VEB 401 209 261 667**[35]

---

[35] Source: http://em.cbonds.com/countries/Venezuela-bond

The number of bonds held by US investments funds had become so high that the US government thought it was a good idea to issue an executive order making Venezuela a national security threat to the US since too much Venezuelan debt had made its way into US funds. A potential default would hurt bad bets and investment funds and could cause a financial tsunami as there are probably 10x+ more derivatives attached to the Venezuelan debt.

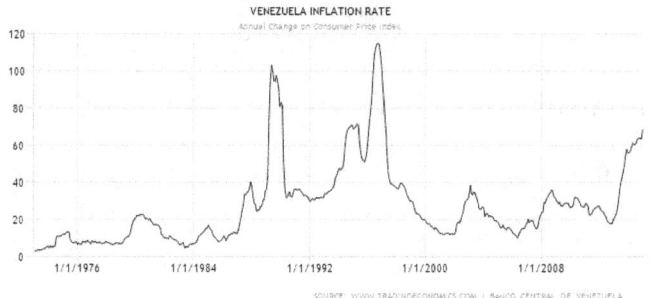

[36]

---

[36] Source http://www.tradingeconomics.com Publicly available numbers

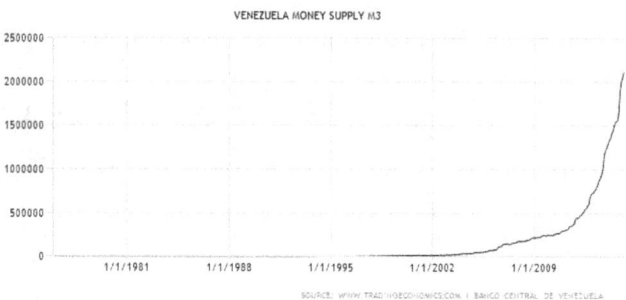

37

The people keep on suffering from bad government policies. Together with fractional reserve banking, once again a country and its people are on the brink of failure and loss of wealth for the 600+ time. As you read this, the current Venezuelan Bolivar may have ceased to exist or ended in hyperinflation, default or even revaluation.

---

[37] **Source** http://www.tradingeconomics.com **Publicly available numbers**

Greece Big Government and the destruction of an economy and its people

Greece is the birthplace of the first debasing of a FIAT currency not in paper form, but in the old form of FIAT precious metal currencies.

The Athenian monetary system was set up in the following way:

6 obols = 1 drachma

100 drachma = 1 mina

600 minae = 1 talent (or the equivalent of 57 pounds of silver)

A skilled worker in Athens could earn about two drachmas a day. Sculptors and doctors were able to make about six drachmas daily. An unskilled worker would make around half a drachma for one day's work.

The typical costs of goods in ancient Greece:

Loaf of bread 1 obol

Lamb 8 drachmas

Gallon of olive oil 5 drachmas

Shoes 8 to 12 drachmas

Slaves 200 to 300 drachmas

Houses 400 to 1000 drachmas

The Greeks' debasement was described in this ancient play of Aristophanes' THE FROGS (405 BC).

Chorus

But if I am correct in discerning the life or the manners of a man, who will yet suffer for it, Cligenes the little, this ape, who now troubles us, the vilest bath-man of all, as many as are masters of soap made from adulterated soda mixed up with ashes, and of Cimolian earth, will not abide for a long time. But though he sees this, he is not for peace, lest he should one day be stripped when drunk, when walking without his cudgel.

The freedom of the city has often appeared to us to be similarly circumstanced with regard to the good and honourable citizens, as to the old coin and the new gold. For neither do we employ these at all, which are not adulterated, but the most excellent, as it appears, of all coins, and alone correctly struck, and proved by ringing everywhere, both among the Greeks and the barbarians, but this vile copper coin, struck but yesterday and lately with the vilest stamp; and we insult those of the citizens whom we know to be well-born, and discreet, and just, and good, and honourable men, and who have been trained in palæstras, and choruses, and music; while we use for every purpose the brazen, foreigners, and slaves, rascals, and sprung from rascals, who are the latest come; whom the city before this would not heedlessly and readily have used even as scape-goats. Yet even now, ye senseless, change your ways and again employ the good. For if you succeed, it will be creditable to you; and if you fail at all, at any rate you will seem to the wise to suffer, if you do suffer aught, from a stick which is worthy.

The Greeks were the first known in history to have government-struck coinage. These coins were over time debased from gold and silver coins to a lesser and lesser valued currency with lesser valued metal in them, but having the same face value. The Greeks ended up with copper coinage at the end of the debasement and the fall of their empire and then they were engulfed by a new empire, The Roman Empire, which had new gold and silver currency.

Today's Greece:

In Greece today there is a big issue of government expenditure which is put into the banking system and then inflated up to 10 times. In Greece the current government spending numbers are 51.9% of its Gross Domestic Product (which is the total goods and services created in a country). This means that the side that has to pay for the government, the private economy with businesses and individuals working in that sector, that 48.1% is less than the size of the government itself. When this happens, the government becomes unsustainable and it implodes.

The Greek government did not have money to provide the services it pledged to the people. So it had to go into debt. It borrowed mostly from ECB, the European Central Bank, and IMF, the International Monetary Fund.

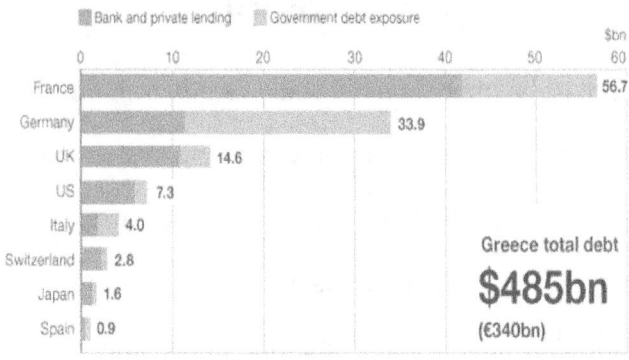

Which used local banks like Deutche Bank and others. Here is an overview over institutions and banks most exposed to Greek debt.

---

[38] Source Bank of International Settlements Quarterly Review 2015

Greece Sovereign Debt Ownership - Top Banks

	Debt Amt (Mln Euro)	% Out
Greece Sovereign Debt Total	275,965.60	100.00%
Total of Bank Holders	**70,744.85**	**25.64%**
Alpha Bank AE	6,139.58	2.22%
Marfin Popular Bank PCL	5,490.96	1.99%
BNP Paribas SA	3,816.00	1.38%
Dexia SA	3,785.00	1.37%
Bank of Cyprus Plc	2,221.28	0.80%
Commerzbank AG	2,200.00	0.80%
Societe Generale SA	1,900.00	0.69%
Deutsche Bank AG	1,154.00	0.42%
Deutsche Postbank AG	923.00	0.33%
Royal Bank of Scotland Group P	832.69	0.30%
Banco Comercial Portugues SA	768.16	0.28%
HSBC Holdings PLC	689.18	0.25%
Banco BPI SA	530.38	0.19%
KBC Groep NV	500.00	0.18%
Credit Agricole SA	326.00	0.12%
Emporiki Bank SA	292.18	0.11%
Attica Bank	255.40	0.09%
Natixis	181.00	0.07%
Landesbank Berlin Holding AG	159.00	0.06%
UBS AG	94.95	0.03%
Barclays PLC	76.40	0.03%
Erste Group Bank AG	74.70	0.03%
Bank of America Corp	6.89	0.00%
Swedbank AB	5.56	0.00%

* Data sourced from company financial statements/Bloomberg 2Q 2011

---

[39] Source Financial Data from http://www.bloomberg.com

Greece Sovereign Debt Ownership - Top Institutions

	Debt Amt (Mln Euro)
Greece Sovereign Debt Total	275,965.60
Total of Top 50 Institutional Holders	4,101.59
AMUNDI	356.73
LOOMIS SAYLES & COMPANY LP	275.15
ALPHA MUTUAL FUND MANAGEMENT CO	215.53
PARVEST INVESTMENT MANAGEMENT	184.91
DIETHNIKI MUTUAL FUND MGMT	181.75
EUROBANK EFG MUTUAL FUND MGMT	178.93
NATIXIS ASSET MANAGEMENT	172.97
SANPAOLO IMI ASSET MANAGEMENT LU	167.57
EUROBANK EFG MUTUAL FUND MGMT CO	147.26
BNP ASSET MANAGEMENT PARIS	147.09
NATIXIS ASSET MANAGEMENT ADVISOR	117.42
FORTIS INVESTMENT MANAGEMENT SA	116.19
PETERCAM SA	109.71
BNP PARIBAS ASSET MANAGEMENT SGR	101.01
UNION INVESTMENT GMBH	93.56
LBPAM	87.11
JULIUS BAER MULTICOOPERATION	84.71
CLERICAL MEDICAL INVESTMENT GRP	74.80
AMUNDI LUXEMBOURG SA	74.57
PIONEER ASSET MANAGEMENT SA	72.51
ALLIANZ GLOBAL INVESTORS FRANCE	71.51
TT ELTA AEDAK	68.77
UNION INVESTMENT LUXEMBOURG SA	55.50
GENERALI FINANCES	52.45
ROTHSCHILD & COMPAGNIE GESTION	51.49
BLACKROCK GROUP LIMITED	51.44
UNIVERSAL INVESTMENT GMBH	48.61
PETERCAM SA	46.62
ALLIANZ HELLENIC MUTUAL FUND MGM	46.06
ATE MUTUAL FUND MANAGEMENT CO SA	45.55
RIVERSOURCE INVESTMENTS LLC	45.18
ACHMEA BELEGGINSFONDSEN BEHEERNV	44.36
ING PIRAEUS FUND MANAGEMENT	40.08
BLACKROCK FUND ADVISORS	39.62
INVERCAIXA GESTION SA SGII	39.17
ERSTE SPARINVEST KAGMBH	37.43
STATE STREET BANQUE S A	34.91
KEPLER-FONDS KAGMBH	33.38
BBVA GESTION SA SGIIC/SPAIN	32.00
DWS INVESTMENT SA	28.70
ING ASSET MANAGEMENT	27.02
UNIVERSAL INVEST CONSEIL	27.00
FRANKLIN ADVISERS INC	26.00
DWS INVESTMENT GMBH	24.05
BPI FUNDOS GFIM SA/PORTUGAL	22.61
HWANG-DBS INVESTMENT MANAGEMENT	22.55
COVEA LUX FONDS SPECIAL	22.50
RENTA 4 GESTORA SGIIC SA/SPAIN	20.12
BARCLAYS WEALTH MANAGERS SGIIC S	19.25
KBC BANK LUXEMBOURG SA	18.20

* Data sourced from company financial statements/Bloomberg

Then the government programs became so expensive that there was no money left in the private economy to support them. The only way the Greek government could operate was by getting into debt from bankers.

As of current June 20th 2015, when I am writing this, the bankers are saying that they don't want to lend them more money. The Greek government is now locked up and is forced to declare bankruptcy. The people will have to pay back in taxation hikes and by selling off assets like commodities and their lands to foreign corporations and global bankers that have lent them the money. This will make them debt slaves. And now by saying that there are no more money to lend, the debt «slave» will become a permanent slave.

The Greek government refuses to see what is happening. They have operated like any other debt slave by getting deeper and deeper into debt to pay off old interest on the original debt in order to stay afloat.

The Government is unsustainable. It should really look at reforming itself and taking its people off the drugs of free money that they had to borrow. The death of a country's government is imminent or the Communists will completely take over with their collectivist ideas of full control!

There are only two options out of this mess: the sustainable approach of the oligarchical elite forfeiting the government and handing it back to the people, allowing for the people to control the government and to remove unnecessary taxes. Secondly, they could do the total opposite and put in place a collectivist state with Communist central planning. Today's Central Banking System is communism. They have just become very good at using propaganda to have us accept living in a controlled state while they slowly take more and more of our freedom away.

The Greek government is bankrupt and they have been that since 2008 when the monetary powers started to tighten their supply of free money by hiking up their interest rate. Instead of finding more money by doing real work (which the government really doesn't do) it tried to steal and take money by force, but there is now no money left as people got into debt and lost their houses and went bankrupt to boot. This was caused by the Greek government's failure to get enough taxes in as the price of their loans went up.

Chapter Three
Government Slaves: Austerity

Austerity as a tool to try to fix the economy. Does it help?

You have probably heard a lot about Austerity measures as they are called by mainstream media.

What is Austerity?

What does Austerity entail?

Here is the definition: **Austerity** is a state of reduced spending and increased frugality in the financial sector. **Austerity** measures generally refer to the measures taken by governments to reduce expenditures in an attempt to shrink their growing budget deficits.

I have always believed that cutting the welfare expenditure will not help a government. The poorest people are the ones dependent on government programs and when they cut the stream of money to the poor they will have nothing more to lose and you will have riots, revolution and turmoil on your hand. What happens is that the rich get richer and the poor get poorer.

In Greece, Italy, Ireland, Portugal, Spain, UK, France and Germany in Europe, there have been Austerity experiments, but have they worked?

Here are some recent headlines to take a look at if Austerity helps the economy:

AUSTERITY TO BLAME FOR 35% SUICIDE SURGE IN GREECE–RESEARCH

SHOCKING AUSTERITY: GREECE'S POOR LOST 86% OF INCOME, BUT RICH ONLY 17-20%

ANTI-AUSTERITY PROTESTS ERUPT ACROSS ITALY

THE OPENING OF ECB'S NEW €1B+ HQ SPURRED VIOLENT ANTI-AUSTERITY RIOTS HIT FRANKFURT - PROTESTERS THROW STONES AND SET POLICE CARS ON FIRE AS THE CITY DESCENDS INTO CHAOS

STUDENTS AND RIOT POLICE CLASH DURING ANTI-AUSTERITY PROTESTS IN CITIES ACROSS ITALY

'COSÌ NON VA!': GENERAL STRIKE AGAINST AUSTERITY SWEEPS ITALY

'F**K AUSTERITY': PROTESTERS CLASH WITH COPS OUTSIDE OPENING NIGHT AT LA SCALA, MILAN

THOUSANDS ATTEND ANTI-AUSTERITY PROTESTS IN GREECE, OTHER EUROPEAN CITIES

THOUSANDS RALLY IN SPANISH ANTI-AUSTERITY PROTEST: DEMONSTRATORS GATHER IN THE CAPITAL MADRID DENOUNCING THE GOVERNMENT AND CALLING FOR END TO HARSH AUSTERITY MEASURES.

THE TRUE COST OF AUSTERITY AND INEQUALITY -

PORTUGAL CASE STUDY: AUSTERITY STRETCHES

PORTUGUESE WELFARE SYSTEM TO BREAKING POINT

FOUR REASONS QUÉBEC IS ON THE STREETS FIGHTING

AUSTERITY

VIOLENT CLASHES AS AUSTERITY PROTESTS GRIP EU

CITIES

DESPITE RIOTS, VENEZUELA WILL STRESS

AUSTERITYFROM *(1989)*

INEQUALITY A NATURAL OUTCOME OF AUSTERITY

BANKSTER AUSTERITY MEASURES UNDER ATTACK IN

WAKE OF SYRIZA WIN IN GREECE –

POLITICOS LINE UP FOR FIGHT AGAINST BANKSTER PLAN TO IMPOVERISH MILLIONS

IRISH POLICE DETAIN ANTI-AUSTERITY ACTIVISTS - FOUR ACTIVISTS, ONE A PROMINENT POLITICIAN, FACED QUESTIONING OVER EVENTS AT NOVEMBER PROTEST

FRENCH PRESIDENT FRANÇOIS HOLLANDE'S BUDGET CUTS FORCE MAYORS TO ADJUST –

GOVERNMENT SLASHES FINANCIAL SUPPORT FOR TOWNS AND REGIONS BY $13.8 BILLION

FRANCE HIKES ANTI-TERROR BUDGET DESPITE AUSTERITY COMMITMENT

AUSTERITY PROTESTS TURN INTO ANTI-TURKEY CAMPAIGN IN KKTC

Austerity is not the solution. The solution is full and complete removal of Central Banking and the Commercial Banking system that uses Fractional Reserve Banking.

When you have debt to pay, that will trump all government expenditure. When you have a lot of unfunded liabilities aka welfare programs it doesn't matter if you cut money you still don't have.

What ends up happening is just misery for the people affected by it.

Chapter Four
Bail In: The Real Risk of Having Money In Your Bank Account

Cyprus Bail Ins the start of the banks not being liable for using your hard earned money to bet on derivative casinos

The Cyprus Bail In. The awakening that your deposits in your bank is not yours. It is lent to the bank and they have now an IOU to you! During the Cypriot bail in bank accounts were stolen by banks who made bad bets with the money you thought you had.

In Cyprus, a bet on derivatives by Cypriot banks on failure of Greek debt which ended up being bailed out. The Cypriot bank lost all their money! The next step was something not seen before - a direct looting of their depositors' bank accounts. People lost up to 80% of the money in their bank accounts. Even depositors that had under the insured amount of €100k. Many of them lost up to 30-50%. They of course got shares in the new banks created as an attempt of making them feel better, but having shares in a business that just failed is usually a loss of your money waiting to happen.

CENTRAL BANK OF CYPRUS
EUROSYSTEM

11 February 2013

Mr Takis Phedias
Acting Chief Executive Officer
Laiki Bank

Dear Mr Phedias,

Following the publication of an article in the Financial Times dated 10 February 2013 and titled "Radical rescue proposed for Cyprus", the Central Bank of Cyprus wishes to stress that any action aimed at reducing, depriving or restricting the property rights of depositors, contradicts the provisions of the Constitution of the Republic of Cyprus and of Article 1 of the First Protocol of the European Convention of Human Rights, provisions which protect the right to own property and which are crucial to the functioning of a free market economy.

Hence, any suggestion to the contrary is not only legally unfounded but it cannot merit serious consideration.

Yours sincerely,

Dr George M. Georgiou
Head of Governor's Office
and Communications

After the Cypriot Bail In, other countries were quick to add this legislation in order to save the "Tax" payers from looting, but you need to remember those taxpayers losing money in the bail outs are exactly the same people that would suffer from Bail Ins.

Here is an exert from the Canadian 2013 Action Plan budget:

could cause a disruption to the financial system and, in turn, negative impacts on the economy. This requires strong prudential oversight and a robust set of options for resolving these institutions without the use of taxpayer funds, in the unlikely event that one becomes non-viable.

The Government intends to implement a comprehensive risk management framework for Canada's systemically important banks. This framework will be consistent with reforms in other countries and key international standards, such as the Financial Stability Board's *Key Attributes of Effective Resolution Regimes for Financial Institutions*, and will work alongside the existing Canadian regulatory capital regime. The risk management framework will include the following elements:

- Systemically important banks will face a higher capital requirement, as determined by the Superintendent of Financial Institutions.

144 ECONOMIC ACTION PLAN 2013

Supporting Jobs and Growth
Helping Manufacturers and Businesses Succeed in the Global Economy

- The Government proposes to implement a "bail-in" regime for systemically important banks. This regime will be designed to ensure that, in the unlikely event that a systemically important bank depletes its capital, the bank can be recapitalized and returned to viability through the very rapid conversion of certain bank liabilities into regulatory capital. This will reduce risks for taxpayers. The Government will consult stakeholders on how best to implement a bail-in regime in Canada. Implementation timelines will allow for a smooth transition for affected institutions, investors and other market participants.
- Systemically important banks will continue to be subject to existing risk management requirements, including enhanced supervision and recovery and resolution plans.

This risk management framework will limit the unfair advantage that could be gained by Canada's systemically important banks through the mistaken belief by investors and other market participants that these institutions are "too big to fail."

Supporting the Financial Sector's Contribution to the Economy   41

---

[41] Source http://www.budget.gc.ca/2013/doc/plan/budget2013-eng.pdf

To put in example of what happened during the stealing of money - an old retired lady was selling her retirement property in Cyprus to move back to UK to live with her family. She had £500k and 50% of her money was lost. This was most of her life savings stolen by bankers who made a bad bet without her consent!

Other countries that have prepared bail in strategies like Canada are the Eurozone and New Zealand. By putting this legislation into place they are preparing for a big bank failure. Here is what you need to understand!

If you have your bank in "Your Bank Account" you have given the bank full authority to use your money to do whatever they want without your consent! The money you put in your bank account has now become an IOU and is not really your money again until you withdraw it from your account and stuff it into your mattress. The failure of people not being educated about the monetary system allows the bankers to raise and destroy our wealth!

Talk about getting screwed over by your government for trusting both your government and bankers!!!

Chapter Five
The Rise of The Corporate Fascism: Collusion and The Rise of Monopolies

The rise of Profiteering and Money making Money. The rise of military industrial complex, GMOs in foods, big pharma, big oil and prisons for profit caused by our monetary system!

At one point a Fiat Currency based economy combined with fractional reserve banking ends up becoming non-dependent on human beings. We can see that in today's economy - unemployment is on the rise and corporations start making money by buying back their stocks and borrowing money to pay dividends, and the CEO's only focus is on how to raise profit for the shareholders.

«Competition is always a good thing. It forces us to do our best. A monopoly renders people complacent and satisfied with mediocrity.»
Nancy Pearcey

Today if you don't make money with money you will lose. If you can't beat the hidden tax of inflation created by bankers and governments, you are done. Earlier, it was enough to save up for your retirement, but today you can't just save your money. It needs to grow. That is why you hear economists, businesses, finance ministers and bankers talk about growth. If human beings cannot grow the source of funding at the pace of the debt accumulation with new interest the system will fail and you will get massive bankruptcies as the unsecured debt system will collapse on itself. Who wins here are the big players - bankers and big corporations and they will become bigger and bigger until you have a monopoly. Today we have a couple of sectors of the economy that are using money to make money, cutting corners, keeping us from being healthy, starting wars, increasing the size of government and keeping us in prisons by illegalizing things.

The topic of how each of these sectors are notorious breakers of laws and how their criminal activity was forced to grow by the underlying monetary system.

The Military Industrial Complex

Military companies have one business plan - to sell weapons that kill and intimidate. And when in a monetary system that forces it to grow, it is quite apparent what would happen. In a speech, the former President of the United States of America, Dwight D. Eisenhower, warned against the rise of the

Military Industrial Complex. Well, after his speech, the US has been in dozens of wars and the number increases by the day. The business of these companies is to keep the war going and grow or go bust. What do you think they will do? Keep forcing war upon all of us to make a profit.

Here are the big 20 military companies:

Rank	Company	Country	Arms sales (US$ m.)	Total sales (US$m.)	Arms sales as a % of total sales
1	Lockheed Martin	United States	35,490	45,500	78
2	Boeing	United States	30,700	86,623	35
3	BAE Systems	United Kingdom	26,820	28,406	94
4	Raytheon	United States	21,950	23,706	93
5	Northrop Grumman	United States	20,200	24,661	82
6	General Dynamics	United States	18,660	31,218	60
7	Airbus Group	European Union	15,740	78,693	20
8	United Technologies Corporation	United States	11,900	62,626	19
9	Finmeccanica	Italy	10,560	21,292	50
10	Thales Group	France	10,370	18,850	55
11	L-3 Communications	United States	10,340	12,629	82
12	BAE Systems Inc.	United Kingdom	10,300	11,363	91

Rank	Company	Country	Arms sales (US$ m.)	Total sales (US$m.)	Arms sales as a % of total sales
13	Almaz-Antey	Russia	8,030	8,547	94
14	EADS Cassidian	European Union	6,750	7,936	85
15	Huntington Ingalls	United States	6,550	6,820	96
16	Rolls-Royce	United Kingdom	5,550	24,239	23
17	United Aircraft Corporation	Russia	5,530	6,913	80
18	Safran	France	5,420	19,515	28
19	United Shipbuilding Corporation	Russia	5,120	6,377	80
20	Honeywell	United States	4,870	39,055	12

As you can see from this table, not all of the companies have a main income from arms, but they are feeding the system of war and destruction. Any one of these companies, no matter if they have a very small amount of their income from selling arms, is in my point of view a corrupt company. They profit from millions of people getting killed. Many people grow their wealth by investing in these companies and the results of the company are dependent on how big wars can get created.

Do you think anyone should make profits from wars? Well, whether you like it or not, these companies make money for every bomb dropped on human beings or every bullet fired that kills someone. Should we let the controllers of money, the bankers, force this system to grow even further? I don't think we should!

Big Agra/Food Corporations

It is all about better yields and faster growth of food in order to feed the system of growth. In the last 30 years, Big Agra has grown the same way. The companies have grown bigger and eventually ended up becoming monopolies. Big agriculture companies invented genetically....

manipulated organisms and pesticides that kill everything except for the food that get doused in it. These companies have been blamed, and many times rightly so, for increase in cancer and other diseases like ALS and other neurological diseases. I am not going to go into the details, but there is recent proof.

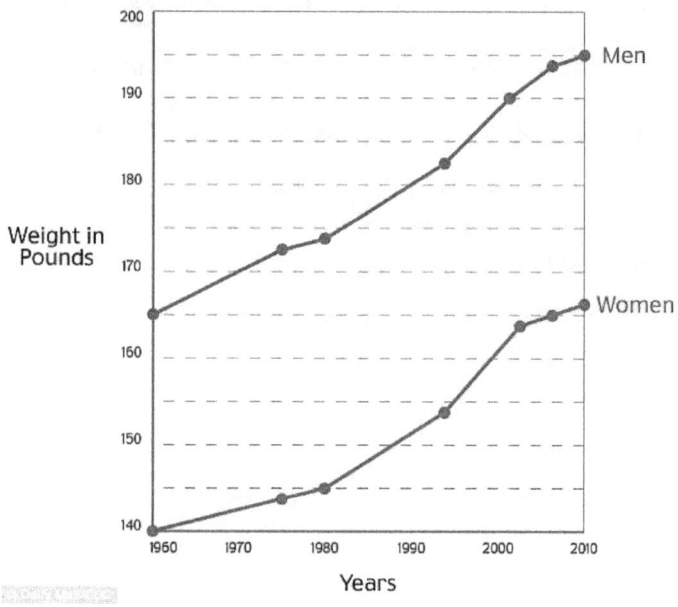

"The scientists behind a recent World Health Organization study which concluded the herbicide glyphosate "probably" causes cancer, say they stand behind their assessment. The comments come in response to criticism from Monsanto Co., who said the study was based on "junk science". The main ingredient in Monsanto's Round Up product is glyphosate. Monsanto executives said they are reviewing their options as they move forward".[42]

What about Aspartame that's used in diet drinks and many other food products linked to obesity and other diseases like Brain Tumors, MS, Lymphoma, Alzheimer's and many other diseases? [43]

The thing though is that through the need to profit and grow these companies have come up with ways to manipulate our food and the way we farm, just like the military industrial

---

[42] SOURCE http://www.globalresearch.ca/world-health-organization-wont-back-down-from-study-linking-monsanto-to-cancer/5439840

[43] Source http://articles.mercola.com/sites/articles/archive/2011/11/06/aspartame-most-dangerous-substance-added-to-food.aspx

complex is driven. All to make profits for their shareholders. Big corporations are now manipulating, deceiving and lobbying to keep their power, but as the system deteriorates their power will either become a monopoly or dissolve as people will stand up against these tyrannical organizations in food and agriculture sector. These companies add cheaper things to our food to make it last longer and dangerous compounds to keep food from rotting naturally. An example here is Monsanto's BT Corn, a plant that is a pesticide itself that is linked to numerous dangerous diseases.

As it is very pricey to mass produce good food, derivatives of foods have created a wave of destruction which affects people's health. Here are some charts to consider.

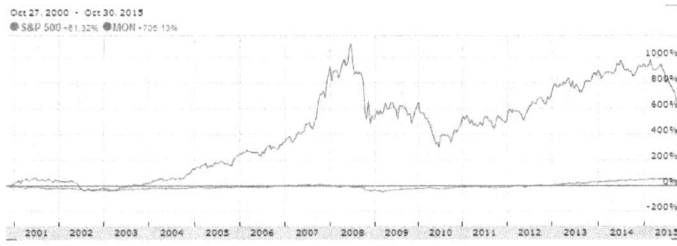

44

All of the big topics I am talking about have a main cause - death and destruction. These topics are grand topics in themselves, but I have chosen to see beyond the corporate walls to a certain what has caused their rise. And as you can see the main driving force is the monetary system.

Companies in the food industry are:

---

[44] Source Interactive Data via FactSet Research Systems

The Big Agra Companies are:

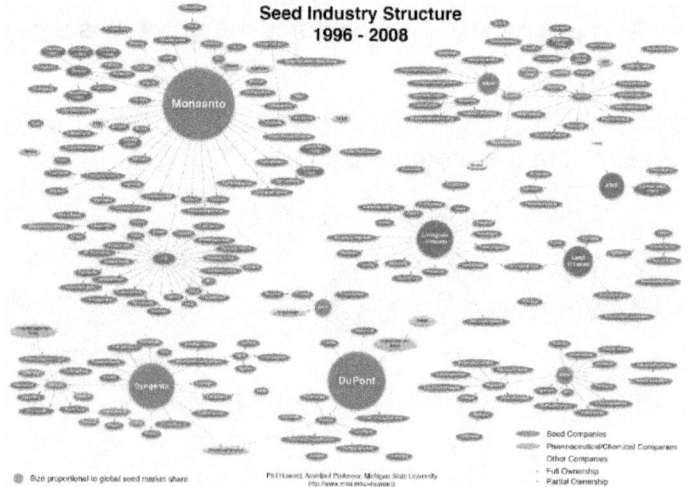

Big Pharma

We have gone through the big food companies that have caused a lot of issues. Well, here comes the cleanup crew - the Pharmaceutical industry. You would think they were there to help you, but if we go deeper into this industry we find a lot of dirty laundry.

The big actors, you would think, would have the good intent of healing you and protecting you from your illnesses. Pharmaceuticals used to be all about the healing, but yet again the monetary system has corrupted the industry. It becomes apparent that all the people fighting all these different industries are fighting a common cause!

It is claimed that many medicines today only hide the real disease and not cure it, therefore giving repeat sales to the companies selling different medicines! I am not saying this without having seen lots of research on this topic. Think about it. How come we haven't cured diseases like cancer? A cure might lie in the above section of the Big Agra and Food industry. I am not an expert in any of these industries, but when you research, it makes you have an opinion on the topic when you look at all the facts and figures.

The pharmaceutical industry is driven by the need to profit and grow. The CEOs of these companies are only loyal to one group of people, and that is their shareholders! They don't care about other human beings' sufferings. They care about the higher profits so they can get bonuses and about giving their shareholders bigger share prices and dividends forced upon them by the ever inflating monetary supply.

You should know who these companies are:

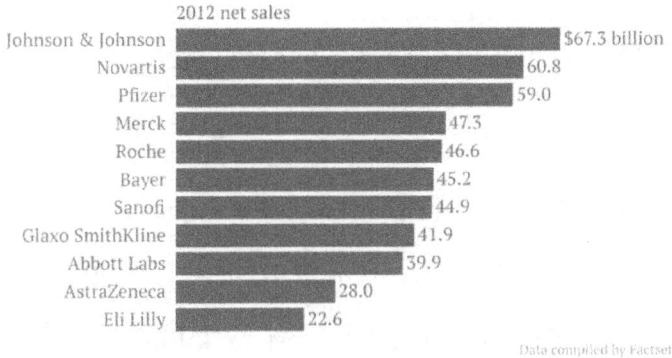

45

As you can see there is a lot of money in keeping you from becoming a healthy human being. Do the research yourself. By looking at how the monetary system works, many experts have pointed this fact out.

Big Oil

There have always been many issues around the big oil companies. The boom in oil as fuel

---

[45] Source FirstWord Dossier

has been able to fuel the massive growth of our system and is a probable cause that has kept the current monetary system alive for so long.

Oil is the single most important commodity today and the oil industry itself has started to suffer as they need profits to raise as debt and interest are killing them slowly.

Again, the corporations only care about their shareholders to give them higher profits on their investments. Many say numerous wars have been fought over getting ever more access to oil to boost shares and dividends to investors, which is needed to keep the ever increasing money supply by stealing from those who invest to keep their savings from getting evaporated as the fiat currency fails.

They have created some of the worst disasters and the pollution from their businesses is causing cancer and deaths everywhere.

Oil has become a way of raging a war on nations that we don't like as they are working on becoming independent and sometimes go against the interests of the main monetary empire - the US.

Company name	Sales (US$ million)
Exxon Mobil	486,255
Royal Dutch Shell	484,489
BP	386,463
Saudi Aramco	311,000
Chevron Corporation	245,621
Conoco Phillips	237,272
Total SA	231,580
Gazprom	157,830
Eni	153,676
Petrobras	145,915

	GDF Suez	126,076
	Pemex	125,344
	Valero Energy	125,095
	PDVSA	124,754
	Statoil	119,561
	JX Holdings	119,258
	Lukoil	111,433
	National Iranian Oil	110,000
	Petronas	97,355
	Indian Oil	86,016
	Repsol	81,122
	PTT	79,690
	Sonatrach	76,100
	Reliance Industries	76,119
	China National Offshore Oil	75,514
	Marathon Petroleum	73,645
	Pertamina	70,924
	Rosneft	65,093
	Company name	**Sales (US$ million)**
	TNK	48,909
	Idemitsu Kosan	48,828
	OMV Group	47,349

Sunoco	45,765
Bharat Petroleum	44,582
Enterprise Products	44,313
GS Caltex	43,280
Suncor Energy	40,231
Hindustan Petroleum	38,885
Hess Corporation	37,871
Centrica	36,860
PKN Orlen	36,100
Ecopetrol	35,520
Hellenic Petroleum	35,495
World Fuel Services	34,623
China National Aviation Fuel	34,352
Plains All American Pipeline	34,275
Cosmo Oil	33,672
Motor Oil Hellas	31,769
Murphy Oil	31,446
Oil and Natural Gas Corporation	30,746
Tesoro	29,927
GasTerra	29,332
Gas Natural	29,305
Ultrapar	29,073
S-Oil	28,808

●	Showa Shell Sekiyu	28,497
🏳	Formosa Petrochemical	27,179
▬	MOL	26,698
☯	Korea Gas	25,721
▬	Surgutneftegas	25,663

Oil and Gas companies have the most power in the world as the second next important thing second to water and food is Oil!

Prison Industrial Complex

Prisons for profit is only in the US, but it is an important topic as it is again fueled by the current monetary system's need for growth to keep the Ponzi scheme alive.

By making something illegal you can now imprison people. That is fine with me if it involves real crimes, but what about incarceration of people for possession of marijuana?

That is another topic, but let's take a look at the driving force behind the illegalization of substances like Marijuana in today's system.

When you combine prisons with making money and then have shareholders as well then you will have a problem. Since the CEO of Corrections Corporation of America needs to pay his shareholders he will makes moves to lobby governments to lay laws that would lead to incarceration of more people.

The following chart should give you a look at what has happened since 1971 when the current global monetary system went full fiat!

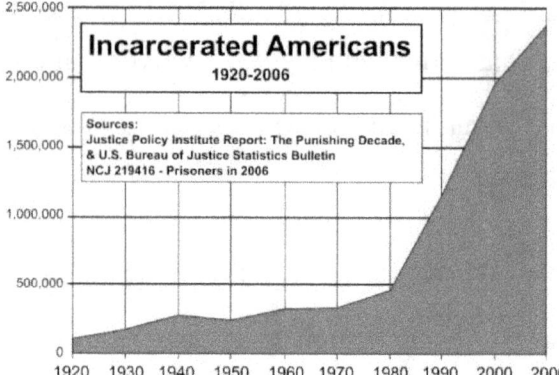

Chapter Six
Interest rate Apartheid: The new black is bad credit

The new era of division comes from giving favourable interest rates on the money borrowed. The problem that has emerged today is people that shouldn't have borrowed money got into trouble and many times went bankrupt because they were chased out of the global economy by limiting their access to money through a rating of their credit worthiness.

This makes the bankers treat you very differently. The reason I call it interest rate apartheid is because the less money you make the more you have to pay to get access to it. And I am not talking about when you invest in real estate. I am talking about when people who barely have money go to a pay day lender and borrow money for 4000% annual interest while the rich people, bankers and corporations borrow money at close to 0% annual interest. Inequality will rise because when we print money, big organizations like JPMorgan, Nestle, BP, Boeing, Goldman Sachs, Alcoa, P&G and many others get the money cheap while they keep us in place by giving us loans for 2-4000%. They can control us by restricting us to a part of the flawed system. They have the ability to create cheap money and buy assets while many companies pay you minimum wage and force you to become dependent on governments and pay day lenders or modern day loan sharks.

We are shrinking as a middle class.

The end product of a failing monetary system based on fiat currency and fractional reserve banking are two classes- RICH and POOR!

Chapter Seven
International Money Fraud

IMF (International Monetary Fund) OR International Money Fraud?

The International Monetary Fund is a bank that can be looked at as a global bank which has planned over decades to create a global currency that can replace trade between nations. The problem with their currency, the Special Drawing Right, is that it is based on a Fiat Currency and Fractional Reserve Banking system which as we have showed above has failed a massive number of times.

The IMF has been known to lend money to nations in distress, but with many clauses in place like sale of national treasures or resources or by privatizing national corporations.

IMF and Austerity Measures: The SDR

The IMF is well known to give loans to many countries who cannot pay them back. They are also known for the clauses they put in place when they lend money to "countries in need".

These clauses are merely a hidden agenda of the IMF to bankrupt or corporatize a nation so their banker friends can make profits.

The many different measures are known as Austerity measures. Austerity means government make cuts in their spending. This only hurts the poor and the wealthier classes who do not receive any support from the government remain mostly untouched. This is a great way for governments to keep you in line and keep begging for more from the government as you cannot afford to buy anything for your daily needs. The IMF is more than willing to give loans to nations. But taking a loan from IMF is comparable to taking loans from loan sharks.

In one of the more recent loans of 5B in Special Drawing Rights, the proposed global currency of the IMF, to Ukraine the IMF broke one of their own rules to lend money to a country at war. That makes the IMF an unofficial Arms Dealer as most of the money would be used to fight the Russian Separatists. The IMF is a western global bank. More recently, the creation of the BRICS development bank and the Asian Infrastructure Investment Bank has created a counterpart to the IMF's global control through lending with Austerity clauses in place.

Will the new Asian banks make the world better?
I don't believe so as they are all running the same old Ponzi schemes of Fractional Reserve Banking and Fiat Currency.
We will probably see more turmoil as these banks compete to suck up assets and steal from

global governments and give back to the corporate elite.

Here are some links that you should read on IMF's involvement in scandals around the globe.

Here are a few articles that might make you think about how good the IMF is. The IMF, throughout its existence, has been blamed for lending money just to loot several countries of their resources and enrich the corrupt elite. The IMF is well known for using Austerity measures in order to lure stupid elite into stealing money from the borrower countries!

Ukraine

https://www.imf.org/external/np/sec/pr/2015/pr15105.htm

http://www.reuters.com/article/2015/03/11/us-ukraine-crisis-imf-idUSKBN0M71D620150311

https://www.imf.org/external/country/ukr/ http://www.globalresearch.ca/whats-behind-ukraines-secret-weapons-deal-with-the-united-arab-emirates-uae/5433309

Greece

http://www.imf.org/external/np/exr/facts/glance.htm

https://www.imf.org/external/np/sec/pr/2012/pr1285.htm

http://www.bloomberg.com/news/articles/2015-02-02/greece-seeks-third-debt-restructuring-who-s-on-the-hook-

http://www.ibtimes.co.uk/imf-introduces-0-05-interest-rate-floor-sdr-loans-reserves-1471687 http://www.google.ca/url?sa=t&rct=j&q=&esrc=s&source=web&cd=39&cad=rja&uact=8&ved=0CPABEBYwJg&url=http%3A%2F%2Fwww.minfin.gr%2Fsites%2Fdefault%2Ffiles%2Fcr1257.pdf&ei=OuUAVciDJsvuoAS7g4LICQ&usg=AFQjCNHHo1IJqoecEnIg8IlVMhUfP-5Uhg&sig2=CaX7k7KsKpVIw7gG5ViShQ

And many others have borrowed money from the IMF who gladly shares money with everyone, with clauses attached of course.

http://www.ipsnews.net/2008/11/indonesia-saying-no-thank-you-to-imf-loans/

http://www.publicfinanceinternational.org/features/2014/11/imf-approves-emergency-loan-for-Guinea-Bissau/

http://www.economist.com/blogs/freeexchange/2011/07/international-monetary-fund

http://blogs.wsj.com/middleeast/2013/06/09/imf-approves-loan-for-tunisia-now-comes-the-reforms/

http://www.bbc.com/news/business-29387821 http://www.rte.ie/news/business/2014/1120/66 0914-sweden-imf-loans/

http://www.bne.eu/content/story/imf-postpones-bosnia-loan-tranche-over-lack-reform

http://allafrica.com/stories/201502271738.html

http://www.balkaninsight.com/en/article/serbia-strikes-loan-deal-with-imf

http://www.imf.org/external/np/fin/tad/extarr11.aspx?memberKey1=ZZZZ&date1key=2020-02-28

http://www.larouchepub.com/other/2001/2847imf_bankrpt.html

http://old.jamaica-gleaner.com/gleaner/20091028/business/business9.html

http://www.kyivpost.com/opinion/op-ed/imf-loans-only-deepen-unchecked-corruption-bankrup-96876.html

http://www.modernghana.com/news/219270/1/imf-and-world-bank-agents-of-poverty-or-partners-o.html

http://www.pbs.org/newshour/making-sense/former-imf-chief-economist-simon-johnson-loans-wont-help-ukraine/

https://www.globalpolicy.org/component/content/article/209/42926.html

https://www.greenleft.org.au/node/22258 http://www.thecornerhouse.org.uk/resource/exporting-corruption-0

https://books.google.ca/books?id=BreCBAAAQBAJ&pg=PA141&lpg=PA141&dq=imf+loan

s+and+corruption&source=bl&ots=adtpXxRotI&sig=JPHuQtuMyj7_G90F8ELFnSrlESo&hl=en&sa=X&ei=K-kAVeWBJ4LVoASymYDwBQ&ved=0CLUBEOgBMBg#v=onepage&q=imf%20loans%20and%20corruption&f=false

http://law.bepress.com/expresso/eps/126/

Look at all these articles above and it will become apparent to you that the IMF and its way of lending money is just another way of globalizing fraud!

When talking about the IMF and its corrupt lending platforms it becomes important to go all the way to the top of the banking chain in the world today. Many experts have said that the IMF's Special Drawing Rights currency, since its inception in 1969, is a currency that plans to take over world trade by big corporations and government as national fiat currencies fail and become pegged to it like currencies are to the US Dollar today.

Here are the current global holdings of IMF's Special Drawing Rights by countries. Did you know your country had them?

General and Special SDR Allocations
(in millions of SDRs)

Member Country	General SDR Allocation	Special SDR Allocation	Total Millions
Afghanistan, Islamic State of	120.0	8.6	128.6
Albania *	36.1	10.3	46.5
Algeria	930.1	139.4	1,069.5
Angola *	212.2	60.8	273.0
Antigua and Barbuda *	10.0	2.5	12.5
Argentina	1,569.4	132.2	1,701.7
Armenia *	68.2	19.8	88.0
Australia	2,399.2	213.5	2,612.6
Austria	1,388.0	169.3	1,557.3
Azerbaijan *	119.3	34.3	153.6

Bahamas, The	96.6	17.6	114.2
Bahrain	100.1	18.1	118.2
Bangladesh	395.3	67.9	463.3
Barbados	50.0	6.3	56.3
Belarus*	286.4	82.2	368.6
Belgium	3,413.9	424.2	3,838.1
Belize*	13.9	4.0	17.9
Benin	45.9	3.9	49.8
Bhutan*	4.7	1.3	6.0
Bolivia	127.1	10.3	137.4
Bosnia-Herzegovina	125.4	15.0	140.4
Botswana	46.7	6.4	53.1
Brazil	2,250.7	277.7	2,528.4
Brunei Darussalam*	159.5	44.0	203.5
Bulgaria*	474.6	136.3	610.9
Burkina Faso	44.6	3.5	48.2
Burundi	57.1	3.1	60.2
Cambodia	64.9	3.6	68.5
Cameroon	137.7	15.1	152.8
Canada	4,721.6	487.2	5,208.8
Cape Verde	7.1	1.4	8.5
Central African Republic	41.3	2.8	44.0
Chad	41.5	2.7	44.2
Chile	634.6	60.3	695.0
China	5,997.3	755.6	6,752.9
Colombia	573.8	50.3	624.1
Comoros	6.6	1.2	7.8
Congo, Dem. Republic of	395.1	29.4	424.5
Congo, Republic of	62.7	7.3	70.0
Costa Rica	121.6	11.2	132.8
Cote d'Ivoire	241.1	32.0	273.1
Croatia	270.7	32.5	303.1
Cyprus	103.5	9.9	113.4
Czech Republic*	607.4	172.8	780.2
Denmark	1,217.8	134.8	1,352.6
Djibouti	11.8	2.2	14.0

Country			
Dominica	6.1	1.2	7.2
Dominican Republic	162.3	15.0	177.2
Ecuador	224.1	31.3	255.4
Egypt	699.6	63.0	762.5
El Salvador	127.0	11.8	138.8
Equatorial Guinea	24.2	1.3	25.5
Eritrea *	11.8	3.4	15.2
Estonia *	48.3	13.6	62.0
Ethiopia	99.1	17.7	116.8
Fiji	52.1	8.0	60.1
Finland	936.9	110.0	1,046.8
France	7,960.6	1,093.8	9,054.3
Gabon	114.4	18.2	132.6
Gambia, The	23.1	1.6	24.6
Georgia *	111.4	32.5	144.0
Germany	9,643.1	1,205.3	10,848.4
Ghana	273.5	17.3	290.9
Greece	610.1	68.7	678.8
Grenada	8.7	1.6	10.2
Guatemala	155.8	17.4	173.2
Guinea	79.4	5.5	84.9
Guinea-Bissau	10.5	1.9	12.4
Guyana	67.4	5.2	72.6
Haiti	60.7	4.1	64.8
Honduras	96.0	8.8	104.8
Hungary *	769.8	221.3	991.1
Iceland	87.2	8.6	95.8
India	3,082.5	214.6	3,297.1
Indonesia	1,541.4	200.1	1,741.5
Iran	1,109.9	72.1	1,182.0
Iraq	881.0	185.1	1,066.0
Ireland	621.5	66.6	688.2
Israel	688.1	88.9	777.0
Italy	5,230.3	643.4	5,873.7

Jamaica	202.7	18.3	221.0
Japan	9,868.9	1,524.4	11,393.3
Jordan	126.4	18.8	145.2
Kazakhstan *	271.1	72.6	343.7
Kenya	201.2	21.5	222.7
Kiribati *	4.2	1.2	5.3
Korea	2,170.0	161.5	2,331.5
Kosovo *	43.7	11.6	55.4
Kuwait	1,023.8	265.0	1,288.8
Kyrgyz Republic *	65.8	18.9	84.7
Lao, People's Dem. Republic	39.2	2.1	41.3
Latvia *	94.0	26.8	120.8
Lebanon	150.5	38.4	188.9
Lesotho	25.9	3.3	29.1
Liberia	95.8	7.2	103.0
Libya	833.0	180.9	1,013.9
Lithuania *	106.9	30.3	137.2
Luxembourg	206.9	22.8	229.7
Macedonia, FYR	51.1	6.2	57.2
Madagascar	90.6	7.2	97.8
Malawi	51.4	3.9	55.4
Malaysia	1,102.0	105.1	1,207.1
Maldives	6.1	1.3	7.4
Mali	69.2	4.3	73.5
Malta	75.6	8.5	84.1
Marshall Islands *	2.6	0.7	3.3
Mauritania	47.7	4.2	51.9
Mauritius	75.3	5.7	81.1
Mexico	2,337.2	224.0	2,561.2
Micronesia, Fed. States of *	3.8	1.0	4.8
Moldova *	91.3	26.4	117.7
Mongolia *	37.9	10.9	48.8

Montenegro *	20.4	5.4	25.8
Morocco	436.0	39.7	475.7
Mozambique *	84.2	24.6	108.8
Myanmar	191.6	10.7	202.3
Namibia *	101.2	29.2	130.4
Nepal	52.9	7.1	60.0
Netherlands	3,826.9	479.4	4,306.3
New Zealand	663.2	49.3	712.4
Nicaragua	96.4	8.7	105.1
Niger	48.8	4.8	53.5
Nigeria	1,299.7	218.6	1,518.2
Norway	1,239.2	156.1	1,395.3
Oman	143.8	28.7	172.6
Pakistan	766.3	52.3	818.6
Palau, Republic of *	2.3	0.7	3.0
Panama	153.2	17.5	170.7
Papua New Guinea	97.6	18.6	116.2
Paraguay	74.1	7.4	81.5
Peru	473.3	45.3	518.6
Philippines	652.3	69.1	721.4
Poland *	1,014.9	289.8	1,304.6
Portugal	643.0	110.1	753.2
Qatar	195.6	43.0	238.6
Romania	763.7	145.1	908.8
Russia *	4,407.4	1,264.4	5,671.8
Rwanda	59.4	3.7	63.1
Samoa	8.6	1.3	9.9
San Marino *	12.6	2.9	15.5
Sao Tome and Principe	5.5	1.0	6.5
Saudi Arabia	5,178.4	1,308.5	6,487.0
Senegal	119.9	10.4	130.3
Serbia	346.7	41.7	388.4
Seychelles	6.5	1.4	7.9
Sierra Leone	76.9	5.2	82.1
Singapore	639.4	88.4	727.7
Slovak Republic *	265.0	75.5	340.5

Slovenia	171.8	18.7	190.5
Solomon Islands	7.7	1.5	9.3
Somalia	32.8	4.2	36.9
South Africa	1,385.1	179.9	1,565.1
Spain	2,260.2	268.6	2,528.8
Sri Lanka	306.5	18.1	324.6
St. Kitts and Nevis *	6.6	1.9	8.5
St. Lucia	11.3	2.5	13.8
St. Vincent and the Grenadines	6.2	1.4	7.6
Sudan	125.8	16.1	141.9
Suriname	68.3	12.1	80.3
Swaziland	37.6	4.3	41.9
Sweden	1,775.8	226.6	2,002.4
Switzerland *	2,563.8	724.2	3,288.0
Syrian Arab Republic	217.6	25.0	242.6
Tajikistan *	64.5	17.6	82.1
Tanzania	147.4	11.7	159.1
Thailand	802.0	83.6	885.6
Timor-Leste *	6.1	1.6	7.7
Togo	54.4	4.9	59.4
Tonga *	5.1	1.5	6.6
Trinidad and Tobago	248.8	26.1	274.9
Tunisia	212.4	26.1	238.5
Turkey	883.1	75.9	959.0
Turkmenistan *	55.7	14.1	69.8
Uganda	133.8	9.9	143.7
Ukraine *	1,017.1	292.4	1,309.4
United Arab Emirates	453.5	76.2	529.7
United Kingdom	7,960.6	260.6	8,221.1
United States	27,539.1	2,877.0	30,416.2
Uruguay	227.2	16.1	243.3

Uzbekistan*	204.3	58.5	262.8
Vanuatu*	12.6	3.7	16.3
Venezuela	1,971.2	255.1	2,226.4
Vietnam	244.0	23.2	267.1
Yemen, Republic of	180.5	23.0	203.5
Zambia	362.6	38.3	400.8
Zimbabwe	262.0	66.4	328.4
Total³	**161,184.3³**	**21,452.7**	**182,637.0**

Source: IMF Finance Department.[46]

---

[46] IMF Finance Department

The BIS - the Central Bank of the world

There is one current Bank that has more power! The BIS (Bank of International Settlements) works like a Central Bank of all Central banks belonging to not all the countries in the world, but 60 countries in all (G20 countries and 40 others). The bank was established on May 17th in 1930 through an intergovernmental agreement by Germany, Belgium, France, United Kingdom, Italy, Japan, United States and Switzerland. The bank has had some very controversial leaders, between 1933 and 1945 the BIS board of directors included Walther Funk, a prominent Nazi official, Emil Puhl, Hermann Schmitz, the director of IG Farben, and Baron von Schroeder, the owner of the J.H. Stein Bank. In this period, it is alleged that the bank looted assets from Germany.

The BIS sets the rules for all other Central Banks in the 60 countries that it controls legislation of. They, ostensibly, guide the countries' central banks on policies, but with "great responsibility" come all kinds of allegations of corruption and destruction of countries' currencies to help push the IMF's Special Drawing Rights.

All it comes down to if we let the system to be controlled on a global scale we give away all our freedom and we will ultimately lose again as they will push the same flawed economic system.

Here are the members so you can see who this big global central bank influences:

Bank of Algeria, Central Bank of Argentina, Reserve Bank of Australia, Austrian National Bank, National Bank of Belgium, Central Bank of Bosnia and Herzegovina, Central Bank of Brazil, Bulgarian National Bank, Bank of Canada, Central Bank of Chile, People's Bank of China, Bank of the Republic (Colombia), Croatian National Ban, Czech National Bank, National Bank of Denmark, Bank of Estonia, European Central Bank, Bank of Finland, Bank of France, Deutsche Bundesbank, Bank of Greece, Hong Kong Monetary Authority, Hungarian National Bank, Central Bank of Iceland, Reserve Bank of India, Bank Indonesia, Central Bank of Ireland, Bank of Israel, Bank of Italy, Bank of Japan, Bank of Korea, Bank of Latvia, Bank of Lithuania, Central Bank of Luxembourg, National Bank of the Republic of Macedonia, Central Bank of Malaysia, Bank of Mexico, De Nederlandsche Bank, Reserve Bank of

New Zealand, Norges Bank, Central Reserve Bank of
Peru, Central Bank of the Philippines, National Bank
of Poland, Bank of Portugal, National Bank of
Romania, Central Bank of the Russian
Federation, Saudi Arabian Monetary Agency, National
Bank of Serbia, Monetary Authority of
Singapore, National Bank of Slovakia, Bank of
Slovenia, South African Reserve Bank, Bank of
Spain, Sveriges Riksbank, Swiss National Bank, Bank
of Thailand, Central Bank of the Republic of
Turkey, Central Bank of the United Arab
Emirates, Bank of England and the US Federal
Reserve System.

What we need to do is take the power away
from these Central Banks and the Commercial
Banks to create money. That is the number one
we should focus on. The limitations by law on

printing have been broken 100s of times throughout history with the Sung Dynasty's Government printing money even with limitations on the supply of money. The Federal Reserve, or US Central Bank as it should be called, did this by moving away from a gold standard to a fractional gold standard to even less gold backing to full fiat currency with no other backing than the government's force of taxation on you as an individual citizen.

Chapter Eight
The current destruction of currencies: A Global Problem

Our money that we believe has value has become worthless over the last few decades. If you had saved up $10k in the 50s you would have been quite rich, but today having $10k isn't very much. If you have $10k in your retirement account, you wouldn't even last half a year.

Fiat Currencies and Fractional Reserve Banking have been known to destroy wealth 100s of times throughout history, but for some crazy reason today we have implemented the system on a global basis and the International Monetary Fund has a dream to replace the failing system with a global system that's controlled by them.

When will we learn from history that our system is flawed? The system is based on a Ponzi scheme, where those that possess the power of printing this enforced currency gain while those who accept it lose out as the powers that be can print and buy what they want with out-of-thin-air currency, be they assets or weapons.

Here is some collected evidence that money is failing. Take a look at these graphs from Central Banks around the world!

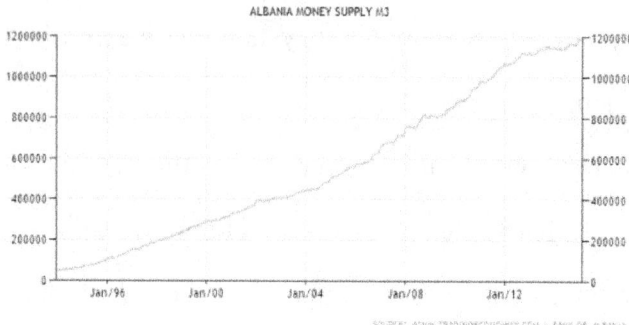

47

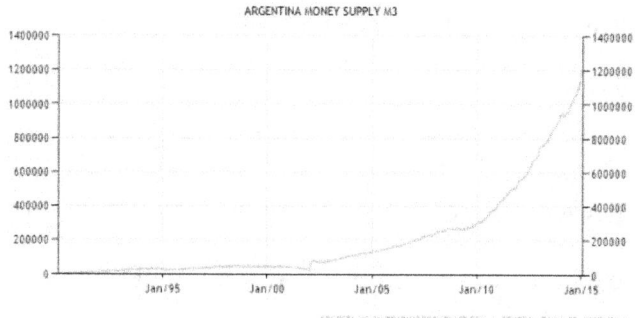

48

---

[47] Source http://www.tradingeconomics.com Publicly available numbers

[48] Source http://www.tradingeconomics.com Publicly available numbers

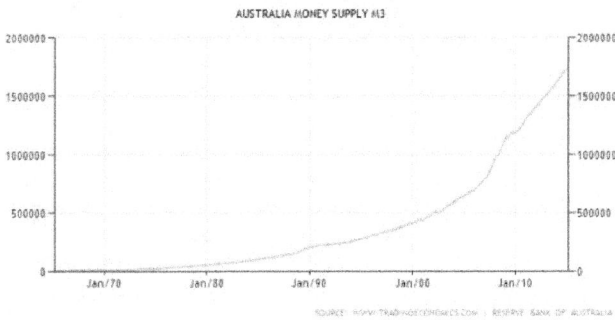

[49]

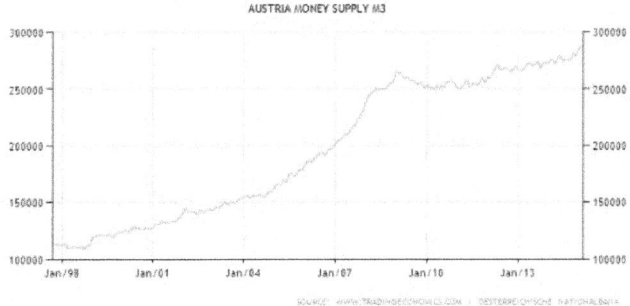

[50]

---

[49] Source http://www.tradingeconomics.com Publicly available numbers

[50] Source http://www.tradingeconomics.com Publicly available numbers

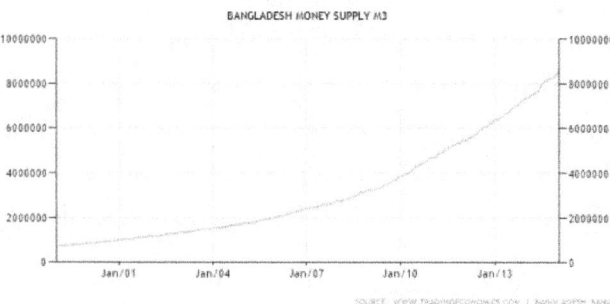

51

52

---

[51] Source http://www.tradingeconomics.com Publicly available numbers

[52] Source http://www.tradingeconomics.com Publicly available numbers

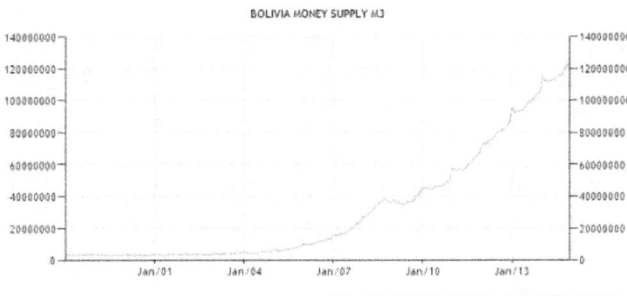

[53]

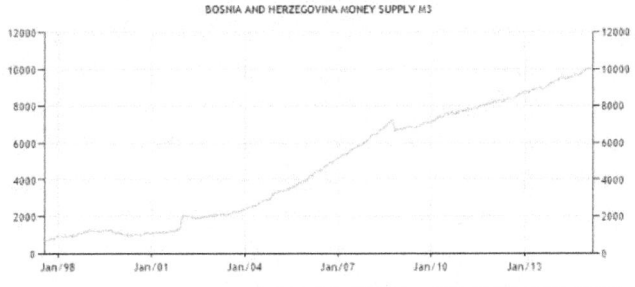

[54]

---

[53] Source http://www.tradingeconomics.com Publicly available numbers

[54] Source http://www.tradingeconomics.com Publicly available numbers

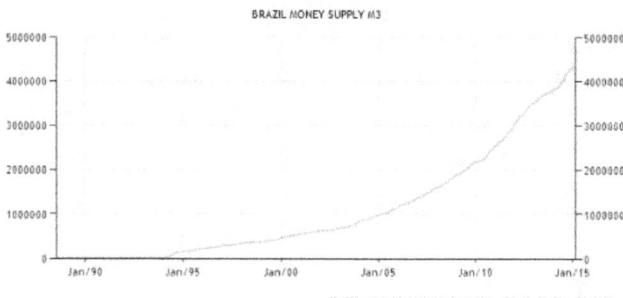

55

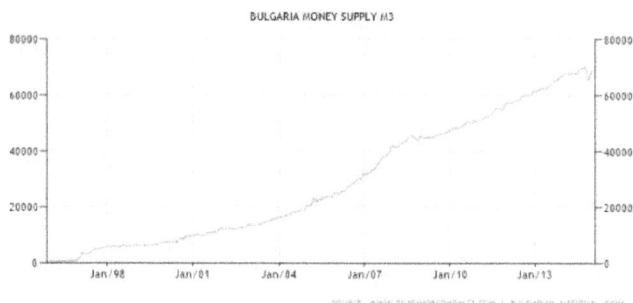

56

---

[55] Source http://www.tradingeconomics.com Publicly available numbers

[56] Source http://www.tradingeconomics.com Publicly available numbers

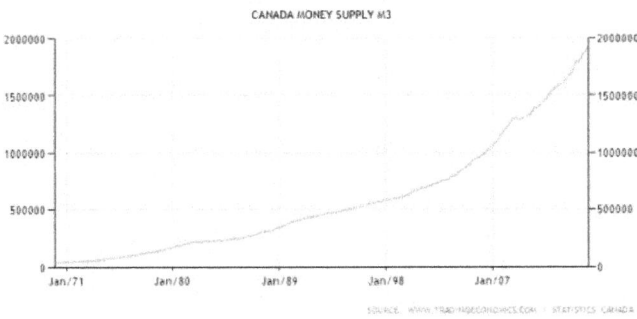

[57]

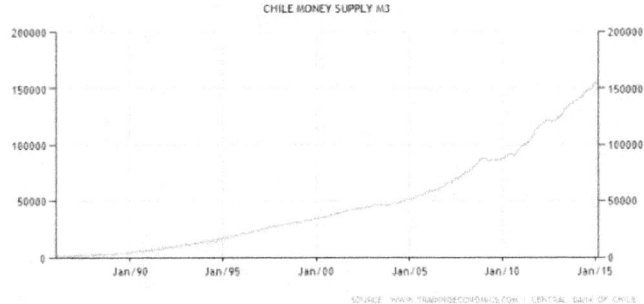

[58]

---

[57] Source http://www.tradingeconomics.com Publicly available numbers

[58] Source http://www.tradingeconomics.com Publicly available numbers

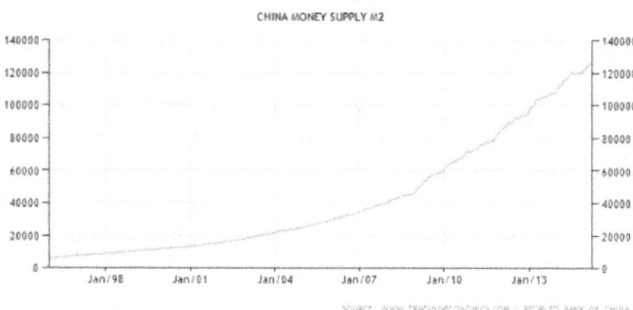

[59]

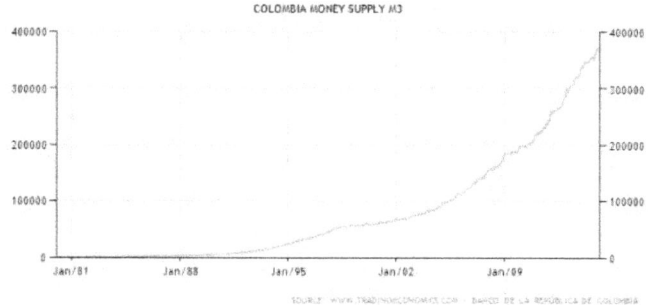

[60]

---

[59] Source http://www.tradingeconomics.com Publicly available numbers

[60] Source http://www.tradingeconomics.com Publicly available numbers

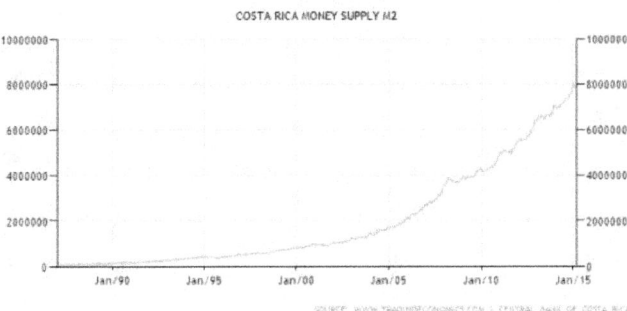

61

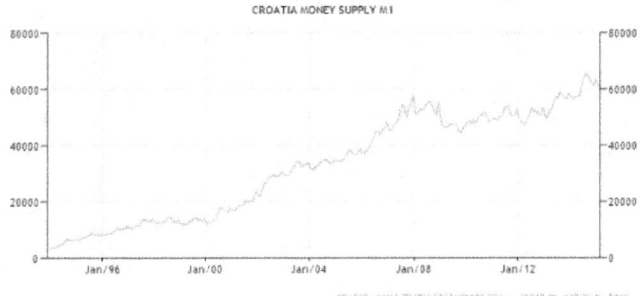

62

---

[61] Source http://www.tradingeconomics.com Publicly available numbers

[62] Source http://www.tradingeconomics.com Publicly available numbers

63

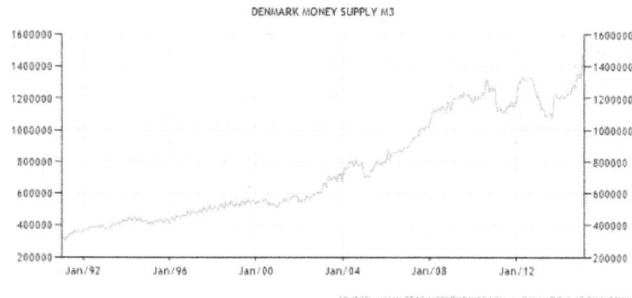

64

---

[63] Source http://www.tradingeconomics.com Publicly available numbers

[64] Source http://www.tradingeconomics.com Publicly available numbers

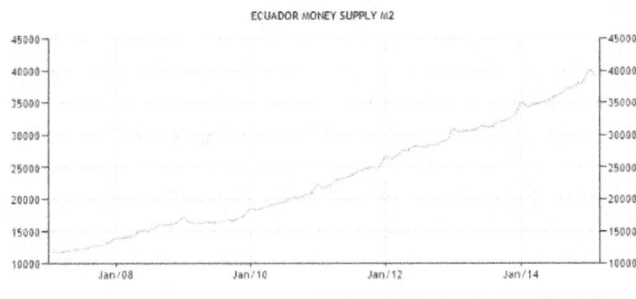

65

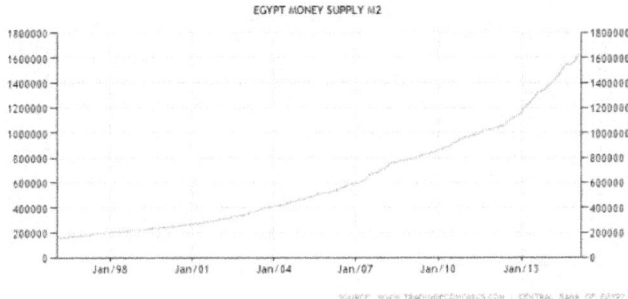

66

---

[65] Source http://www.tradingeconomics.com Publicly available numbers

[66] Source http://www.tradingeconomics.com Publicly available numbers

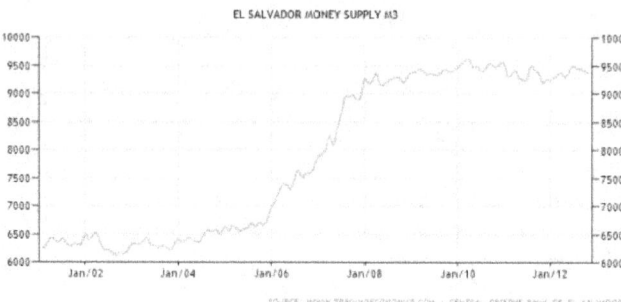

67

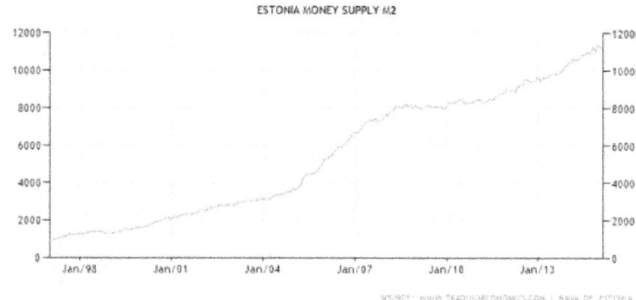

68

---

[67] Source http://www.tradingeconomics.com Publicly available numbers

[68] Source http://www.tradingeconomics.com Publicly available numbers

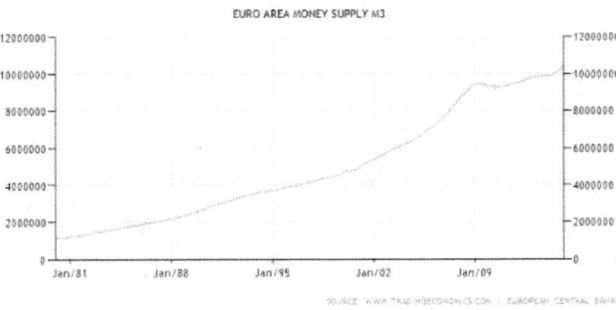

69

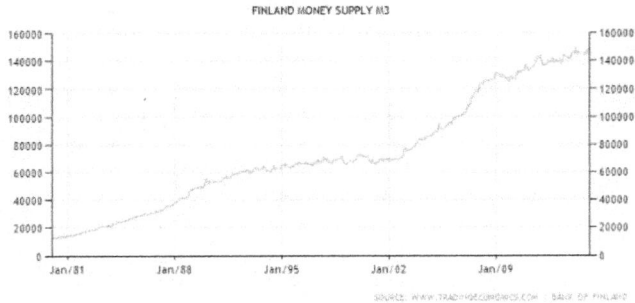

70

---

[69] Source http://www.tradingeconomics.com Publicly available numbers

[70] Source http://www.tradingeconomics.com Publicly available numbers

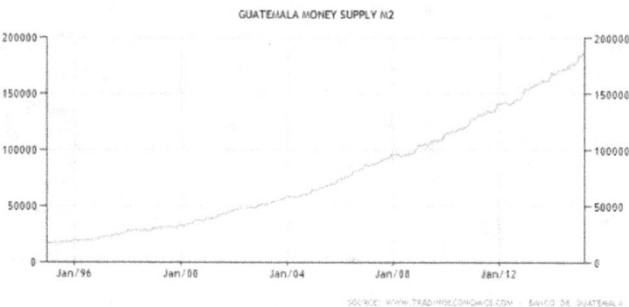

71

72

---

[71] Source http://www.tradingeconomics.com Publicly available numbers

[72] Source http://www.tradingeconomics.com Publicly available numbers

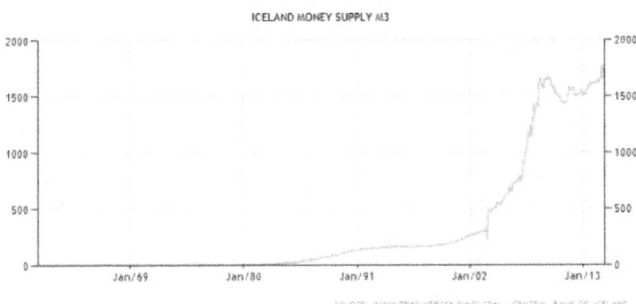

[73]

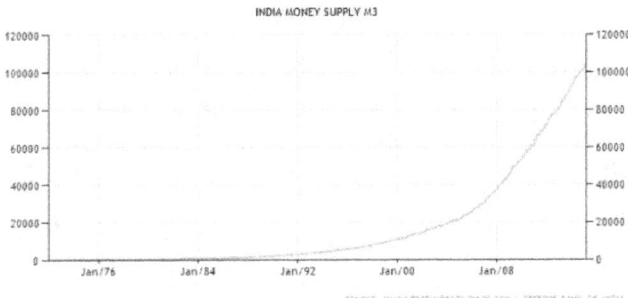

[74]

---

[73] Source http://www.tradingeconomics.com Publicly available numbers

[74] Source http://www.tradingeconomics.com Publicly available numbers

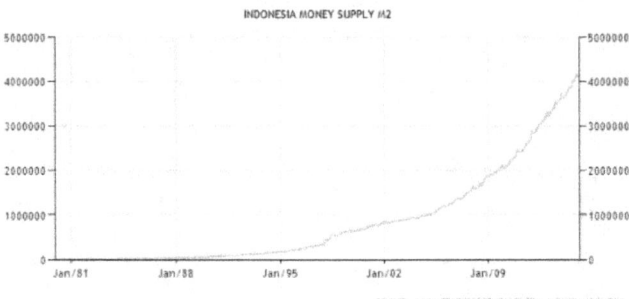

75

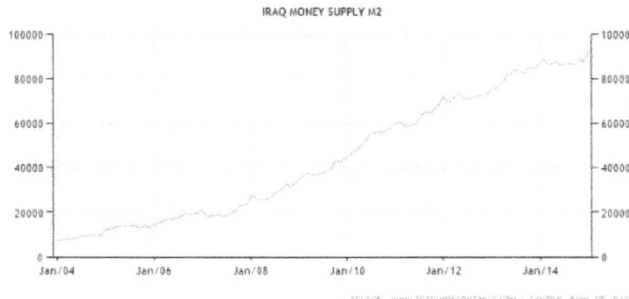

76

---

[75] Source http://www.tradingeconomics.com Publicly available numbers

[76] Source http://www.tradingeconomics.com Publicly available numbers

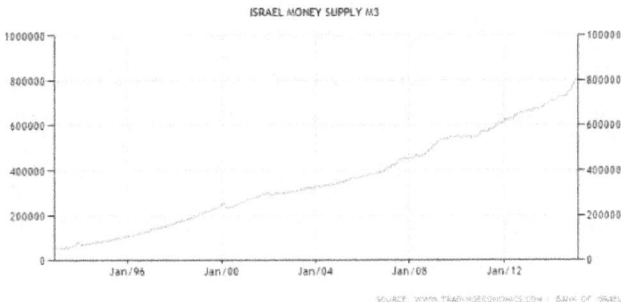

77

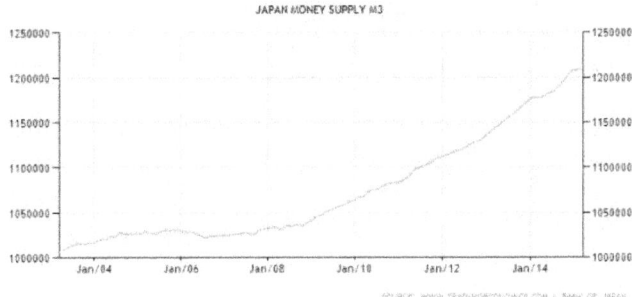

78

---

[77] Source http://www.tradingeconomics.com Publicly available numbers

[78] Source http://www.tradingeconomics.com Publicly available numbers

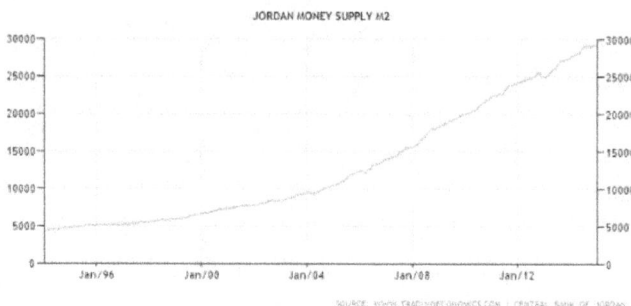

79

80

---

[79] Source http://www.tradingeconomics.com Publicly available numbers

[80] Source http://www.tradingeconomics.com Publicly available numbers

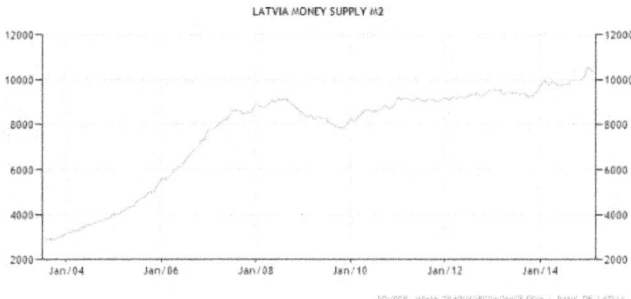

[81]

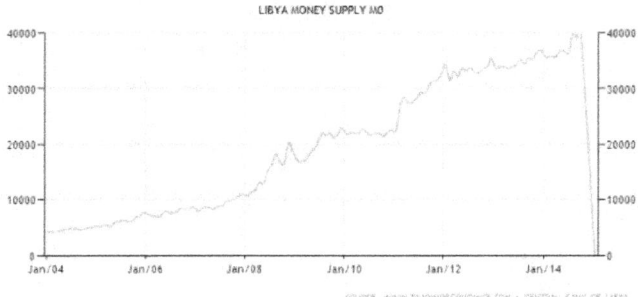

[82]

---

[81] Source http://www.tradingeconomics.com Publicly available numbers

[82] Source http://www.tradingeconomics.com Publicly available numbers

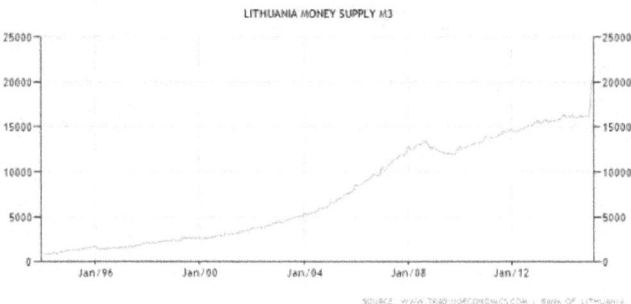

83

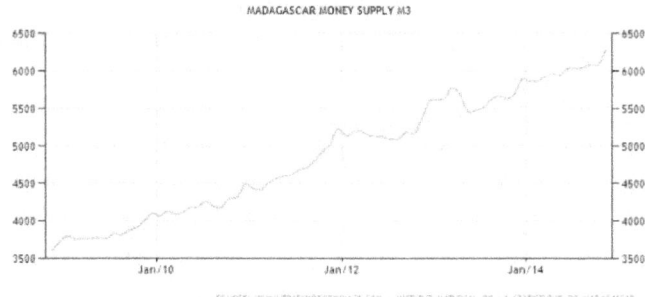

84

---

[83] Source http://www.tradingeconomics.com Publicly available numbers

[84] Source http://www.tradingeconomics.com Publicly available numbers

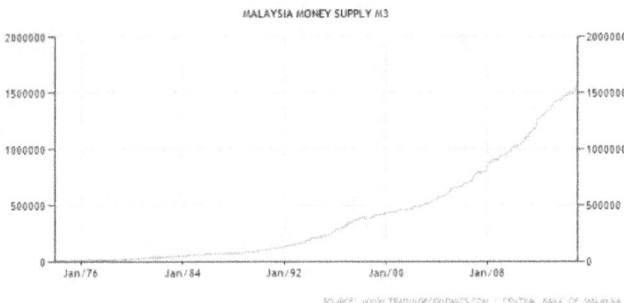

85

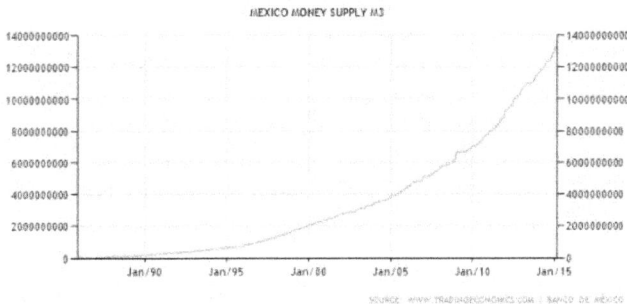

86

---

[85] Source http://www.tradingeconomics.com Publicly available numbers

[86] Source http://www.tradingeconomics.com Publicly available numbers

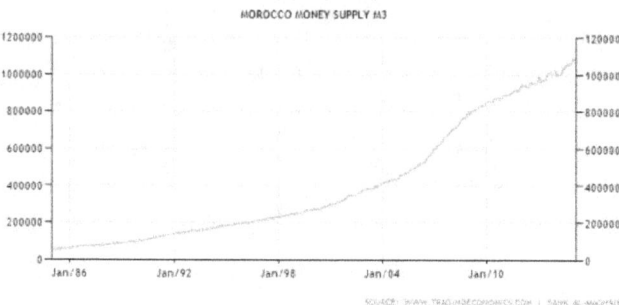

87

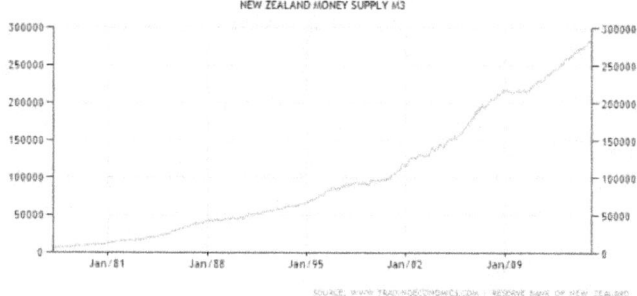

88

---

[87] Source http://www.tradingeconomics.com Publicly available numbers

[88] Source http://www.tradingeconomics.com Publicly available numbers

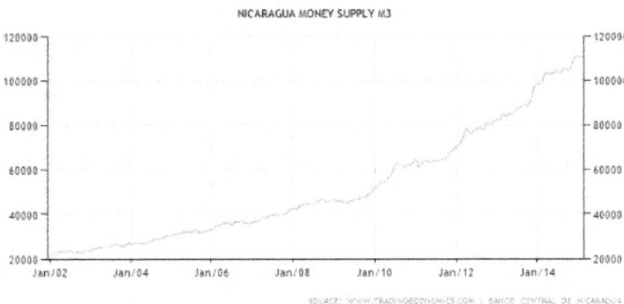

89

90

---

[89] Source http://www.tradingeconomics.com Publicly available numbers

[90] Source http://www.tradingeconomics.com Publicly available numbers

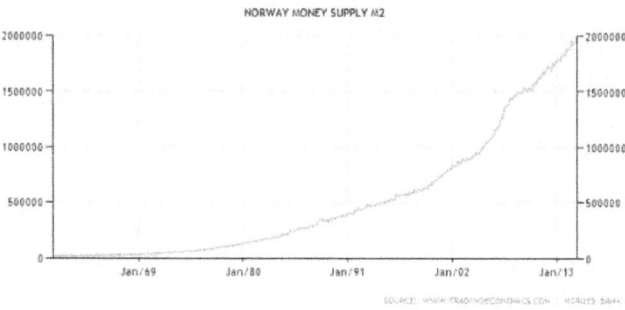

91

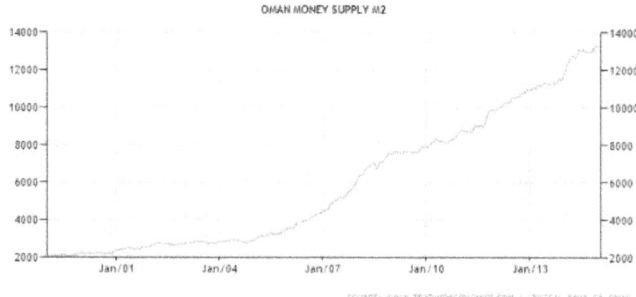

92

---

[91] Source http://www.tradingeconomics.com Publicly available numbers

[92] Source http://www.tradingeconomics.com Publicly available numbers

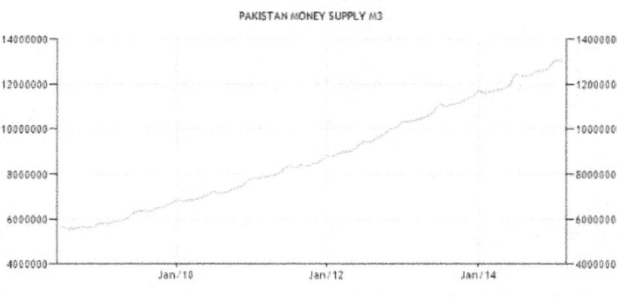

[93]

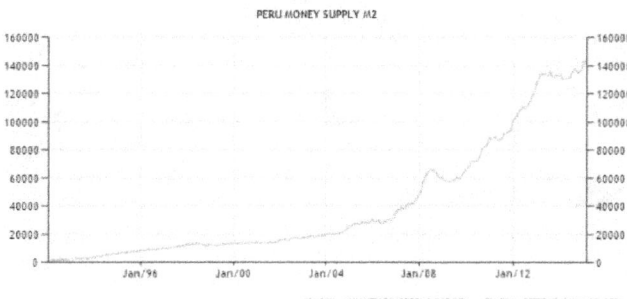

[94]

---

[93] Source http://www.tradingeconomics.com Publicly available numbers

[94] Source http://www.tradingeconomics.com Publicly available numbers

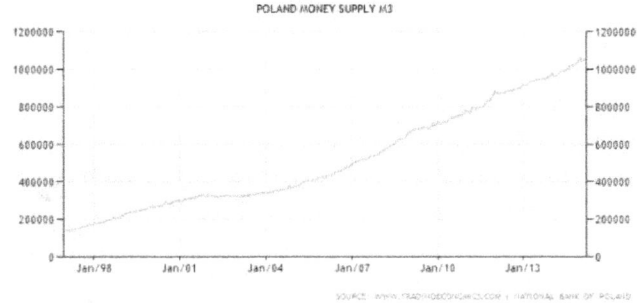

---

[95] Source http://www.tradingeconomics.com Publicly available numbers

[96] Source http://www.tradingeconomics.com Publicly available numbers

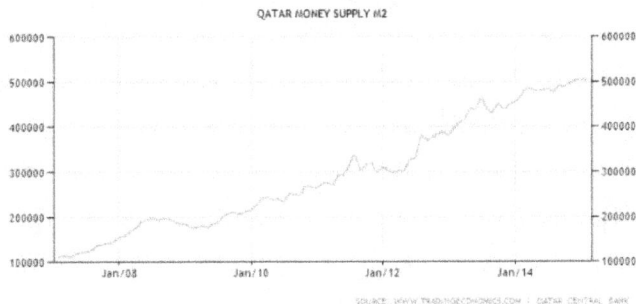

[97]

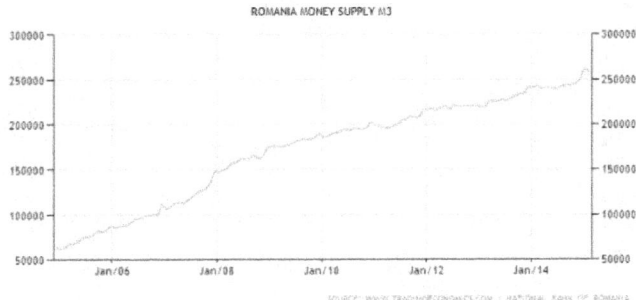

[98]

---

[97] Source http://www.tradingeconomics.com Publicly available numbers

[98] Source http://www.tradingeconomics.com Publicly available numbers

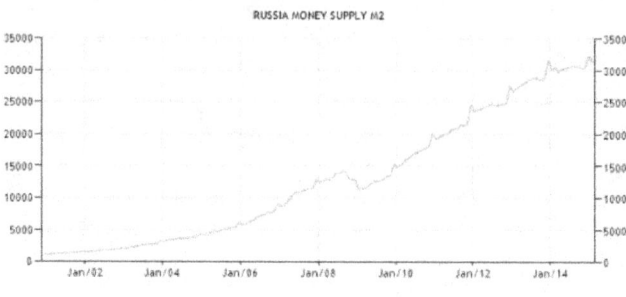

99

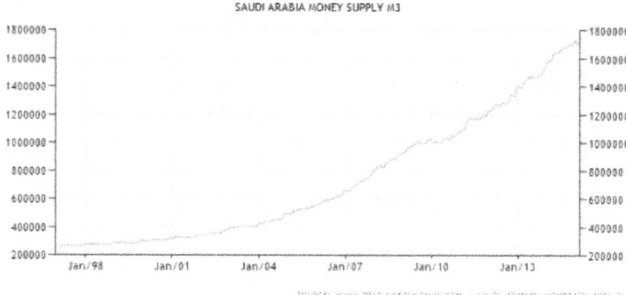

100

---

[99] Source http://www.tradingeconomics.com Publicly available numbers

[100] Source http://www.tradingeconomics.com Publicly available numbers

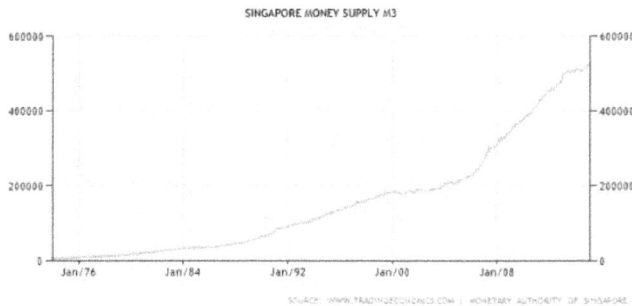

101

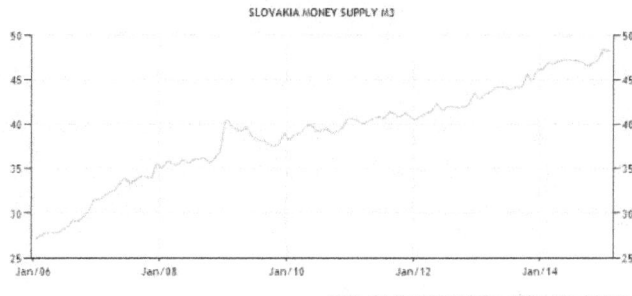

102

---

[101] Source http://www.tradingeconomics.com Publicly available numbers

[102] Source http://www.tradingeconomics.com Publicly available numbers

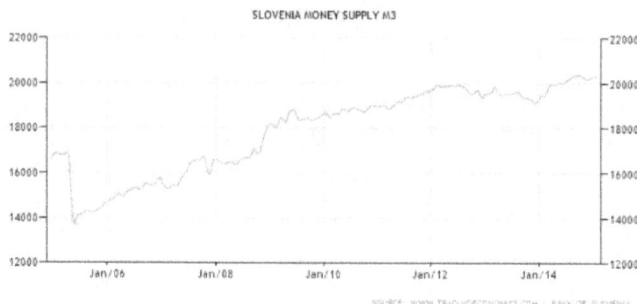

103

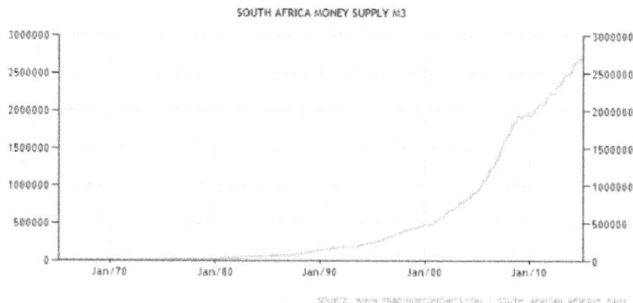

104

---

[103] Source http://www.tradingeconomics.com Publicly available numbers

[104] Source http://www.tradingeconomics.com Publicly available numbers

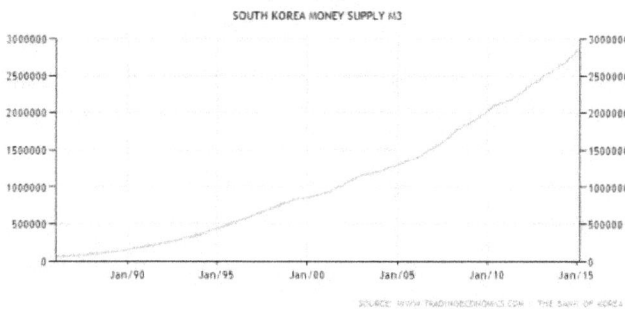

105

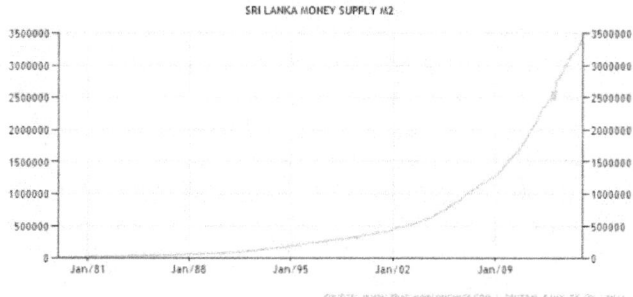

106

---

[105] Source http://www.tradingeconomics.com Publicly available numbers

[106] Source http://www.tradingeconomics.com Publicly available numbers

107

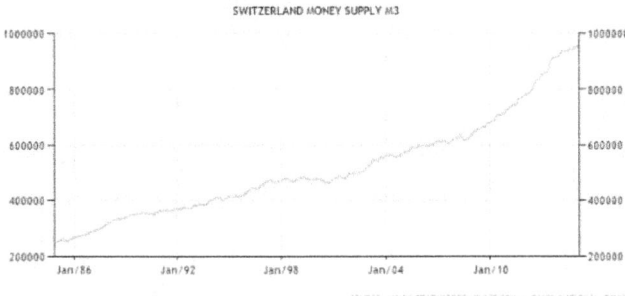

108

---

[107] Source http://www.tradingeconomics.com Publicly available numbers

[108] Source http://www.tradingeconomics.com Publicly available numbers

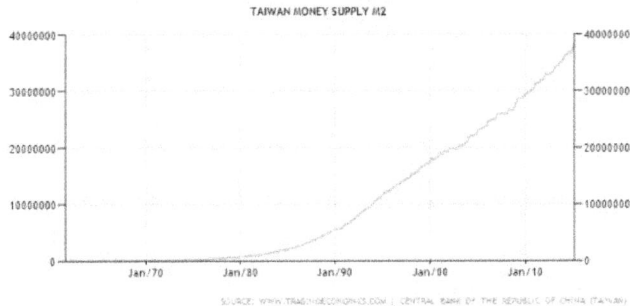

109

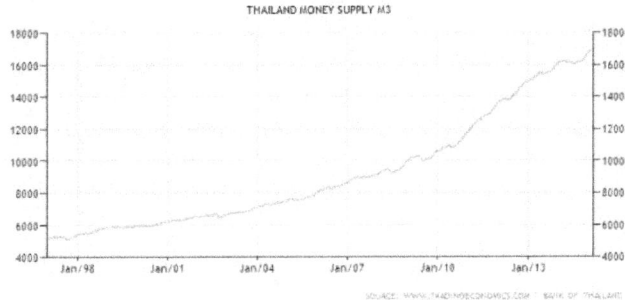

110

---

[109] Source http://www.tradingeconomics.com Publicly available numbers

[110] Source http://www.tradingeconomics.com Publicly available numbers

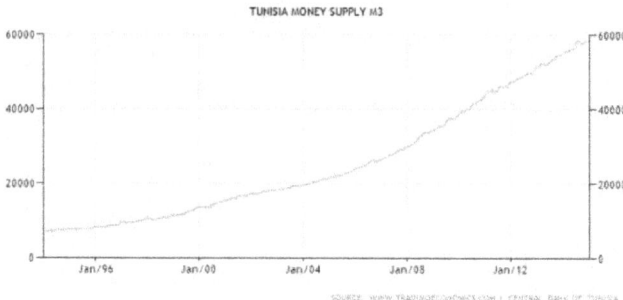

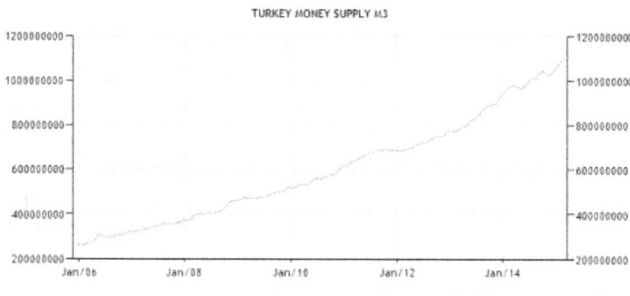

---

[111] Source http://www.tradingeconomics.com Publicly available numbers

[112] Source http://www.tradingeconomics.com Publicly available numbers

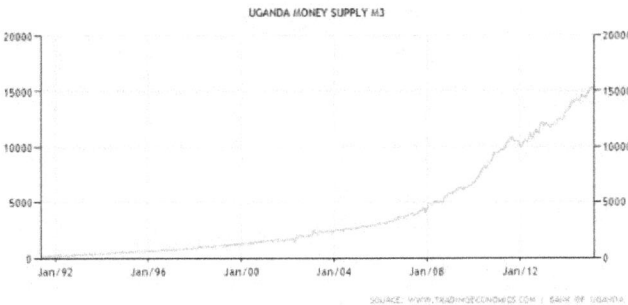

113

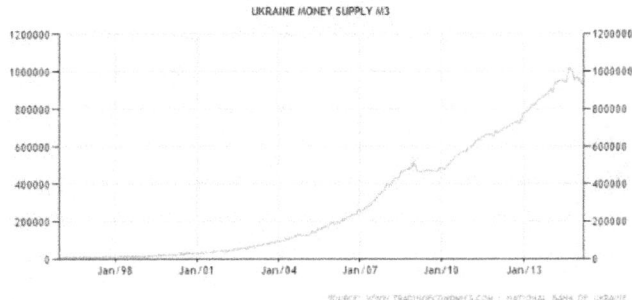

114

---

[113] Source http://www.tradingeconomics.com Publicly available numbers

[114] Source http://www.tradingeconomics.com Publicly available numbers

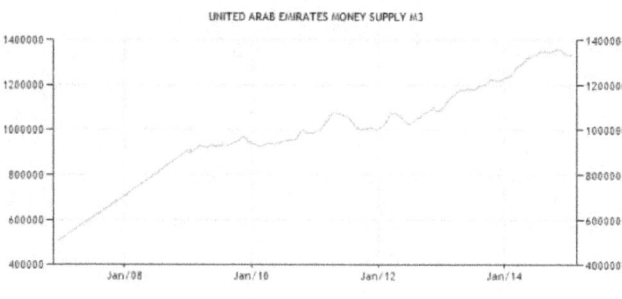

115

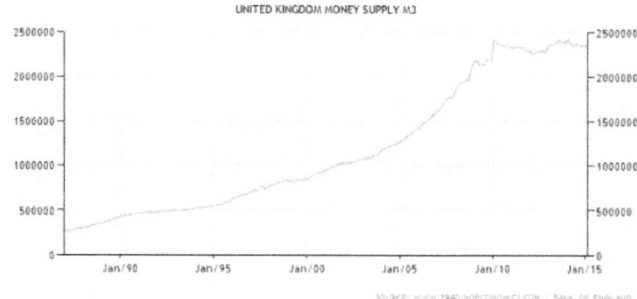

116

---

[115] Source http://www.tradingeconomics.com Publicly available numbers

[116] Source http://www.tradingeconomics.com Publicly available numbers

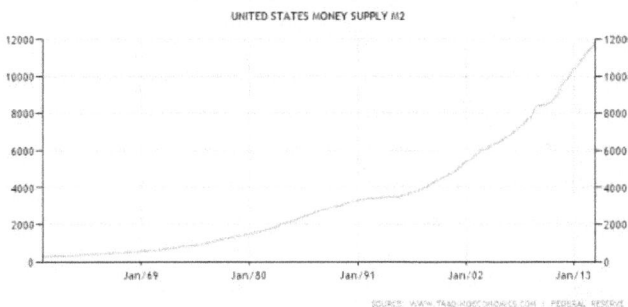

---

[117] Source http://www.tradingeconomics.com Publicly available numbers

[118] Source http://www.tradingeconomics.com Publicly available numbers

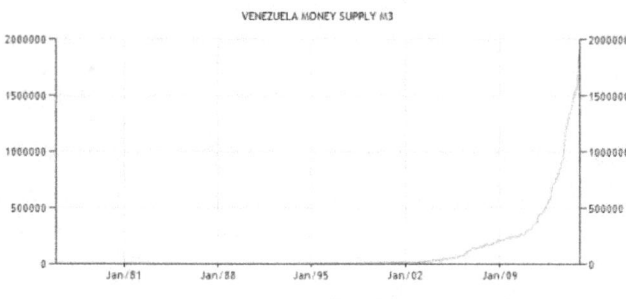

119

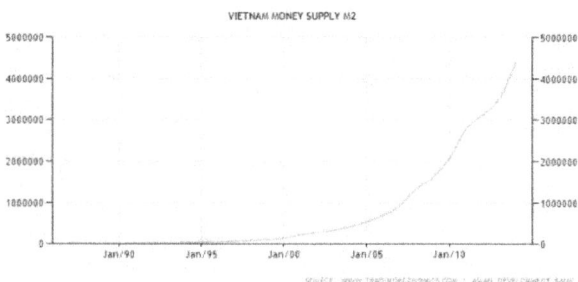

120

---

[119] Source http://www.tradingeconomics.com Publicly available numbers

[120] Source http://www.tradingeconomics.com Publicly available numbers

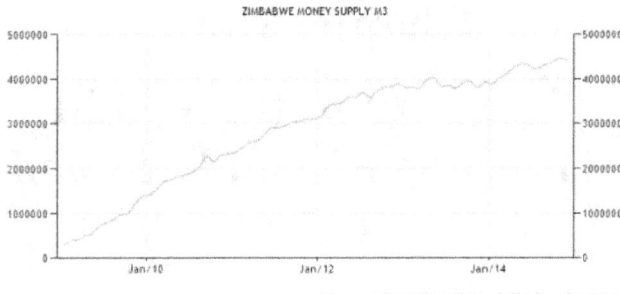

[121] Source http://www.tradingeconomics.com Publicly available numbers

Chapter Nine

The Death of the Middle Class: The Rise of Rich and Poor

Let's take a look at how inequality has exploded since 1971 when the world went off the gold standard.

As you can see in these charts the same thing is happening today as we are getting stolen from by inflation of the money supply and we are becoming poor while the rich and the elite are becoming richer. The bankers, investors, big corporations and government officials are winning while we who work for a living are losing as our earned money is worth less and less with passing time.

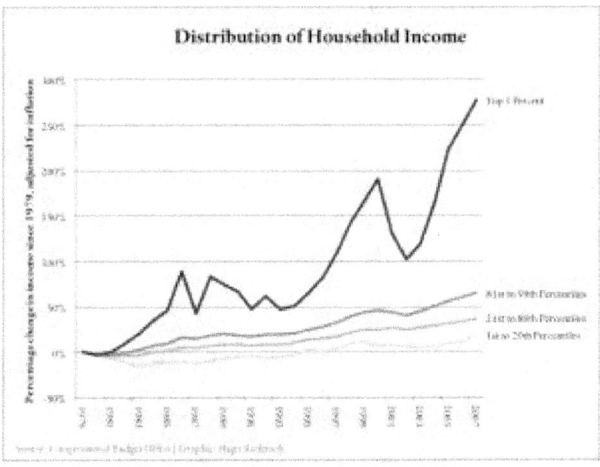

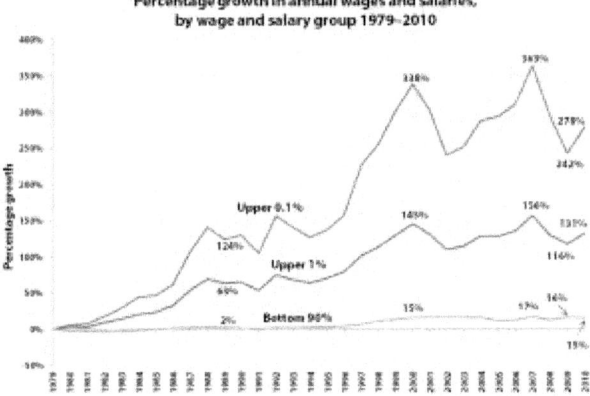

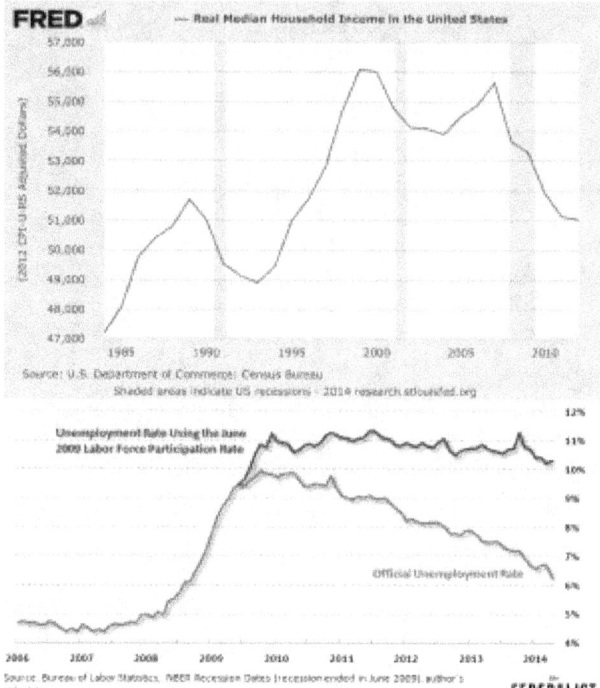

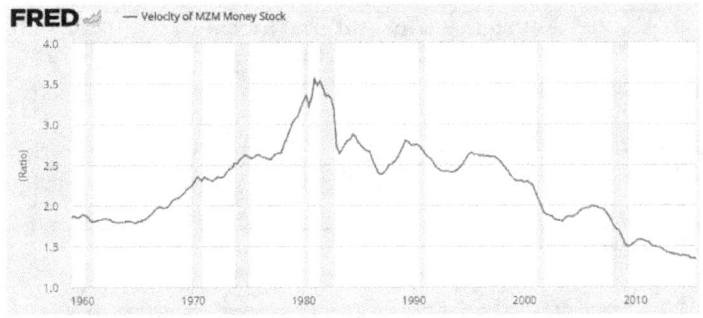

Percentage increase in consumer prices since the first quarter of 1978

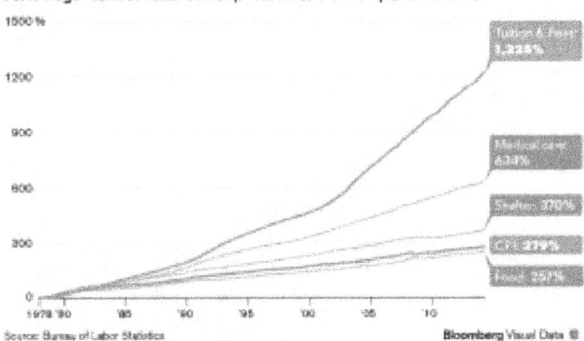

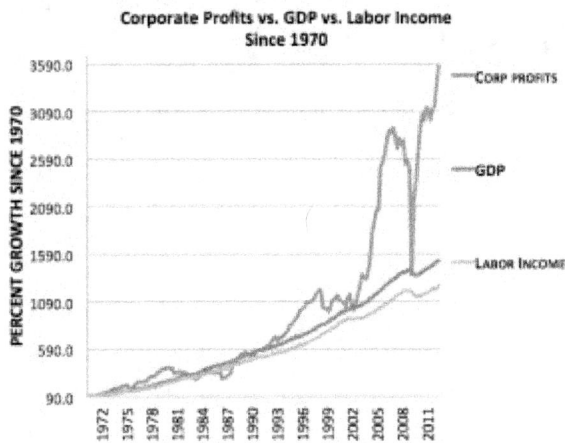

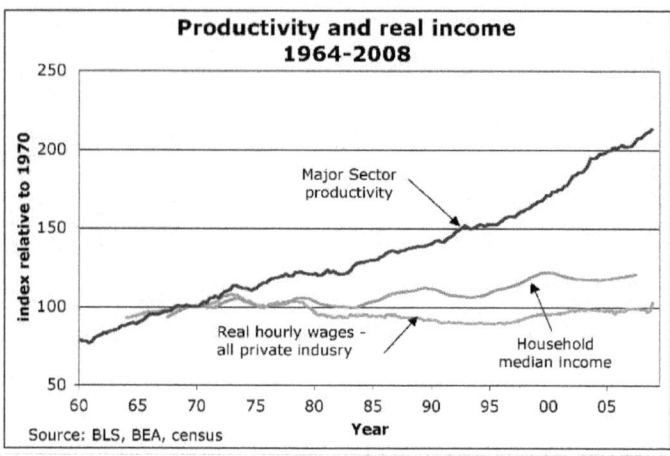
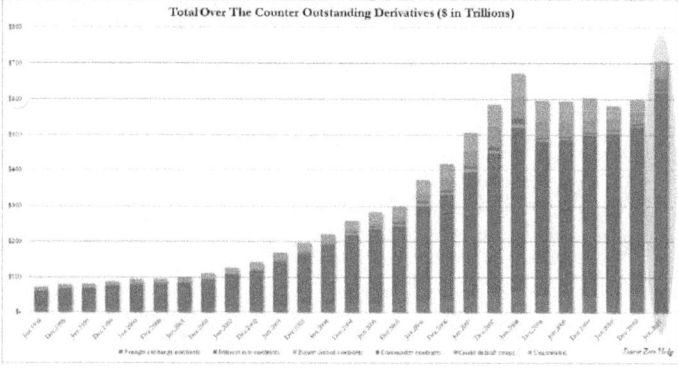

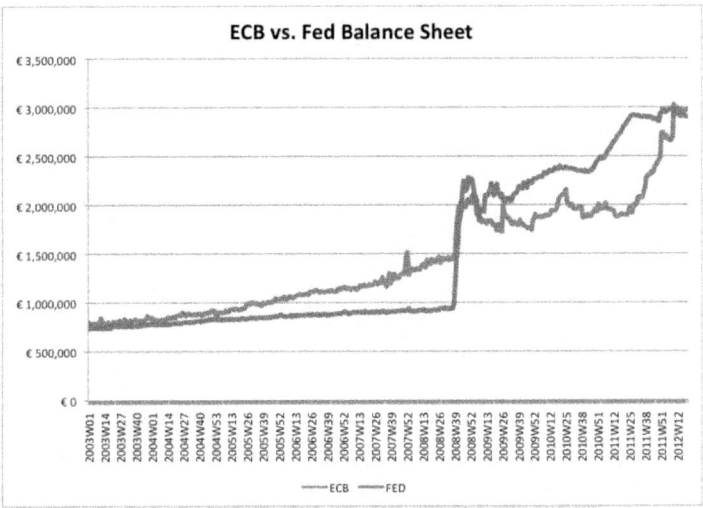
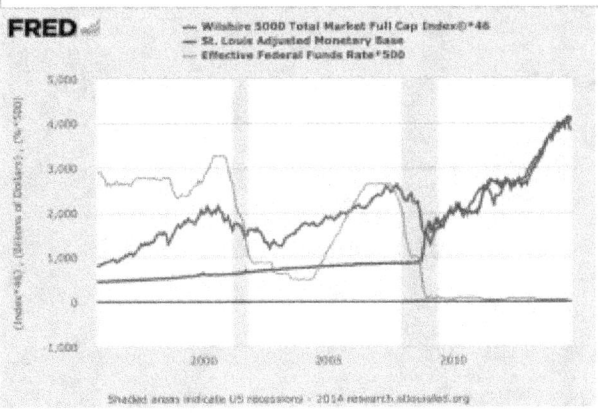

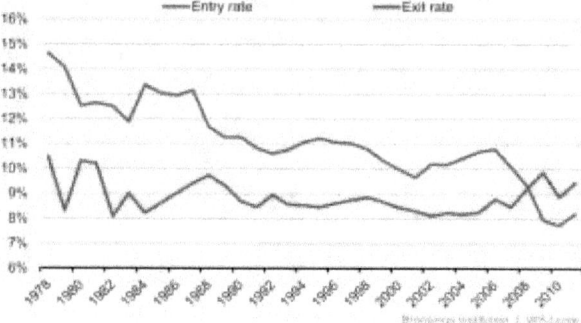

More Companies Closing Than Opening
Percent of all firms each year that form (entry rate) and percent that close (exit rate).

Conclusion

The problem with Fiat Currency and Fractional Reserve Banking

The pictures below are an example of how Fiat Currency was brought into existence by the Central Bank through government borrowing and when that money hit the banking system how Fractional Reserve Banking multiplied the money almost tenfold.

Here is an example of how the system works today in the US, which has the world's reserve currency that is used for trading commodities in many countries today. But it is losing its position as world reserve currency. The Government of the US issues debts to spend on their unfunded liabilities like Medicare, Medicaid, Obama care, social security and food stamps. And on government infrastructure projects. The government creates debt in form of different types of bonds and sell those to investors through major banks in the banking system. By selling these bonds to the Federal Reserve, the US Central bank creates money out of thin air and deposits it into the government's bank account.

The newly created money now ends up in the banking system where it takes a life of its own. Here is what happens.

2
10% Reserve
$100 Bank Deposit
Needs legally a percentage between deposits and new money

$10 Reserve $90 Excessive reserve

$90 created on top of $100

You now have created
$190

Let's say $100 dollars of new money that's been created out of thin air from the FED's magic bank account is deposited into the banking system. The bank takes 90% of it and create an excessive reserve. It is not $90 of the $100, but what the bank does is it lets out a $10 reserve from the $100. The new $90 does not come from the $100, but it gets created out of thin air on top of the $100 deposited into the bank's account from the government. There is now $190 in existence from nothing at all.

3

$90 Bank Deposit

$9 Reserve $81 Excess Reserve

New money created $271

We are not done there. In the next example, the new $90 starts to flow through the banking system and starts getting multiplied. The $90 created as an excessive reserve can now be loaned out to someone who, though cannot afford it, is buying a car or a house, or anything else, it doesn't matter. The same happens again!

The bank takes a $9 reserve at 10%, but it creates the new excessive reserve of $81 that it can now lend into the market again. Now only after 2 times, there is $271 in new Fiat Money in existence.

4

$81 Bank Deposit

$8.1 Reserve $72.9 Excess Reserve

New Money Created $349.3

Once again the same happens. The banks have lent the money out to someone. They now deposit it back into the same or another bank and the fractional reserve banking makes magic happen again. Out of the new $81 lent out now the 10% of that gets held back while the bank creates $72.9 in new money. After 3 times of monetary flow, we have $349.3 in existence. Imagine if we talk about the real numbers of today's economy where this happens to billions every month. Remember, we are willingly accepting this currency for our hard labour.

$$\left[\begin{array}{c} \textbf{Total Created from} \\ \textbf{\$100} \\ \textbf{\$999.51} \end{array} \right]$$

I did the math and towards the end of a Fractional Reserve Banking system, there was a creation almost $1000 of new money on top of the $100 borrowed by using the US FED's magic bank account. We haven't even talked about the interest rate that the banks charge on top of this in many countries like Australia, Belgium, Canada, Sweden and the United Kingdom. These countries have no laws telling them to have any backing of the money they create out of thin air and they charge you interest on top of it to force you to work harder and harder as you are drawn deeper and deeper into debt and are unable to pay off.

The Fiat Currency System is backed by nothing of real value. The governments are allowed to issue as much money as they want relying on their citizen's ability to pay taxes is what backs the system. You can clearly see from the charts above that this system has destroyed the real economy.

In the Fractional Reserve Banking system, the scam and Ponzi scheme take a force of their own. Every dollar of the currency printed by governments, or in the US a privately (bank) owned central bank, can be printed into $10 more dollars. And on top of that they charge you interest for borrowing money from them.

Interest on something printed out of thin air is a scam as the interest does not exist until you create value through your work or business to pay it back. The banking system needs to borrow out more and more money in order to pay off the newly created interest if the debt is unsecured and there are no values created.

The new money or M3 or M2 as shown in the slideshow above fully expresses how the debt needs to increase in order to pay off newly accrued interest by having to work for that debt and becoming a slave to it, but the problem with this is that the growth of money needs to be on an exponential basis and at one time there would be no more people in existence to borrow that money. As was shown in 2008 with the housing bust.

Normally a bust like this will remove the currency created as it can never be paid back and companies and over-leveraged banks should go bust, but something unreal happened in 2008.

Bail out of Bankrupt organizations

Bail Outs were taken from the tax payers and given to bankrupt banks, corporations and institutions. A real economy would say you are obsolete as you have been gambling and grown beyond what was monetarily smart. In 2008, though making money by being a productive person or a business that invested in real growth and invention became obsolete. Now making money with money is the thing and we will see even more rapid increase in inequality as the need for creating great things or being a productive human being has become obsolete and you are now not needed to get the Ponzi scheme going.

Einstein famously said, "The only reason for time is so that everything doesn't happen at once." The same is true about debt. Debt was created because everything in economies can't happen at once; in order to sustain ourselves, some future wealth must be brought forward into the present. In order to do that, we create money that doesn't yet exist in the form of debt. We then hope to earn that money in the future through our economic activities and eventually repay it. Hyman Minsky taught us that "[c]apitalism is unstable because it is a financial and accumulating system with yesterdays, todays, and tomorrows."

Debt seeks to bridge that instability through the form of contracts that ultimately rely on the good will of those who sign them. In that light, we can see the real tragedy of negative interest rates: they not only have the perverse effect of reversing the flow of time, but they demonstrate that borrowers are not acting with the good faith incentives normally associated with someone who needs money. Rather than paying forward, borrowers are paying backwards because they are effectively trying to return something they don't want. Such an arrangement renders it impossible for an economy to grow.

On top of all of this people will now try to cash in their retirements as a massive wave of retirees will sell their assets. This works right against the monetary system as it is deflationary. The monetary system needs inflation to stay alive as it needs exponential growth.

So it is game over!

The system is a failure. Let's learn from our hundreds of failures by looking at history. There is plenty of evidence here that shows how devastating our current system is. I do research other economic and non-economic systems and there are plenty of options available.

I strongly suggest you visit my webpage and look here:

http://www.theeconomictruth.org/systems.html

Let's educate ourselves before we start a truly thought-out revolution. We need to understand the options available to us, discuss them, find the best parts from them and then give people the choice of choosing what system they want and to be a part of that society and not force it upon a minority of people.

By educating yourself you will understand the underlying causes of imprisonment in the US, growing unhealthiest around the world and increasing corruption. It all originates from the greed and the control of money in the hands of those that benefit from it. Until we change we will see more and more governmental control, bigger and more corrupt banks, more people dying from illnesses caused by the big agricultural and pharmaceutical industries who are chasing profit as they need growth to keep their head above water from over borrowing from bankers that have corrupted a real, viable economy with their Ponzi Scheme of Fractional Reserve Banking.

What has happened is corruption and derivatizing of money and the destruction of health of our food and the rise of the ability of imprisoning people for profit.

I hope you have enjoyed reading probably the most important book I will ever write and if you need more examples of economic turmoil caused by Fiat Currencies and Fractional Reserve Banking, let me know. I would happily share more with you if you believe I have presented too little evidence.

I want to share this to make the world better and to understand the 1000s of years' old flaw of Usury as the Christians call it or Rheba as the Muslims call it. The charging of interest and the printing of money out of thin air with no physical value measurement against commodities with your currency! The true crime is when government does this as they have no real value attached to the debt that they incur when they borrow to give money away for free on welfare programs with no real value creation. The Government's only income is taxation and fees.

Famous Quotes about Central Banking and Fiat Currency: A Warning from History

*"If the American people ever allow private banks to control the issue of their currency, first by inflation, then by deflation, the banks...will deprive the people of all property until their children wake-up homeless on the continent their fathers conquered.... The issuing power should be taken from the banks and restored to the people, to whom it properly belongs."
– Thomas Jefferson in the debate over the Re-charter of the Bank Bill (1809)*

"I believe that banking institutions are more dangerous to our liberties than standing armies." – Thomas Jefferson

"... The modern theory of the perpetuation of debt has drenched the earth with blood, and crushed its inhabitants under burdens ever accumulating." - Thomas Jefferson

"History records that the money changers have used every form of abuse, intrigue, deceit, and violent means possible to maintain their control over governments by controlling money and its issuance." - James Madison

"If congress has the right under the Constitution to issue paper money, it was given them to use themselves, not to be delegated to individuals or corporations." -Andrew Jackson

"The Government should create, issue, and circulate all the currency and credits needed to satisfy the spending power of the Government and the buying power of consumers. By the adoption of these principles, the taxpayers will be saved immense sums of interest. Money will cease to be master and become the servant of humanity." -Abraham Lincoln

"Issue of currency should be lodged with the government and be protected from domination by Wall Street. We are opposed to...provision [which] would place our currency and credit system in private hands." – Theodore Roosevelt

Despite these warnings, Woodrow Wilson signed the 1913 Federal Reserve Act. A few years later he wrote: *"I am a most unhappy man. I have unwittingly ruined my country. A great industrial nation is controlled by its system of credit. Our system of credit is concentrated. The growth of the nation, therefore, and all our activities are in the hands of a few men. We have come to be one of the worst ruled, one of the most completely controlled and dominated Governments in the civilized world no longer a Government by free opinion, no longer a Government by conviction and the vote of the majority, but a

Government by the opinion and duress of a small group of dominant men." -Woodrow Wilson

Years later, reflecting on the major banks' control in Washington, President Franklin Roosevelt paid this indirect praise to his distant predecessor President Andrew Jackson, who had "killed" the 2nd Bank of the US (an earlier type of the Federal Reserve System). After Jackson's administration the bankers' influence was gradually restored and increased, culminating in the passage of the Federal Reserve Act of 1913. Roosevelt knew this history.

The real truth of the matter is, as you and I know, that a financial element in the large centers has owned the government ever since the days of Andrew Jackson... - Franklin D. Roosevelt
(in a letter to Colonel House, dated November 21, 1933)

"When a government is dependent upon bankers for money, they and not the leaders of the government control the situation, since the hand that gives is above the hand that takes... Money has no motherland; financiers are without patriotism and without decency; their sole object is gain." – Napoleon Bonaparte, Emperor of France, 1815

"The death of Lincoln was a disaster for Christendom. There was no man in the United States great enough

to wear his boots and the bankers went anew to grab the riches. I fear that foreign bankers with their craftiness and tortuous tricks will entirely control the exuberant riches of America and use it to systematically corrupt civilization." Otto von Bismark (1815-1898), German Chancellor, after the Lincoln assassination

"Money plays the largest part in determining the course of history." Karl Marx writing in the Communist Manifesto (1848).

"That this House considers that the continued issue of all the means of exchange – be they coin, bank-notes or credit, largely passed on by cheques – by private firms as an interest-bearing debt against the public should cease forthwith; that the Sovereign power and duty of issuing money in all forms should be returned to the Crown, then to be put into circulation free of all debt and interest obligations..." Captain Henry Kerby MP, in an Early Day Motion tabled in 1964.

"Banks lend by creating credit. They create the means of payment out of nothing." Ralph M Hawtry, former Secretary to the Treasury.

"... our whole monetary system is dishonest, as it is debt-based... We did not vote for it. It grew upon us gradually but markedly since 1971 when the commodity-based system was abandoned." The Earl of Caithness, in a speech to the House of Lords, 1997.

"The bank hath benefit of interest on all moneys which it creates out of nothing." William Paterson, founder of the Bank of England in 1694, then a privately owned bank

"Let me issue and control a nation's money and I care not who writes the laws." Mayer Amschel Rothschild (1744-1812), founder of the House of Rothschild.

"The few who understand the system will either be so interested in its profits or be so dependent upon its favours that there will be no opposition from that class, while on the other hand, the great body of people, mentally incapable of comprehending the tremendous advantage that capital derives from the system, will bear its burdens without complaint, and perhaps without even suspecting that the system is inimical to their interests." The Rothschild brothers of London writing to associates in New York, 1863.

"I am afraid the ordinary citizen will not like to be told that the banks can and do create money. And they who control the credit of the nation direct the policy of Governments and hold in the hollow of their hand the destiny of the people." Reginald McKenna, as Chairman of the Midland Bank, addressing stockholders in 1924.

"The banks do create money. They have been doing it for a long time, but they didn't realise it, and they did not admit it. Very few did. You will find it in all sorts of documents, financial textbooks, etc. But in the intervening years, and we must be perfectly frank about these things, there has been a development of thought, until today I doubt very much whether you would get many prominent bankers to attempt to deny that banks create it." H W White, Chairman of the Associated Banks of New Zealand, to the New Zealand Monetary Commission, 1955.

"Money is a new form of slavery, and distinguishable from the old simply by the fact that it is impersonal – that there is no human relation between master and slave." Leo Tolstoy, Russian writer.

"It is well enough that people of the nation do not understand our banking and money system, for if they did, I believe there would be a revolution before tomorrow morning." Henry Ford, founder of the Ford Motor Company.

"The modern banking system manufactures money out of nothing. The process is, perhaps, the most astounding piece of sleight of hand that was ever invented. Banks can in fact inflate, mint and un-mint the modern ledger-entry currency." Major L L B Angus.

"The study of money, above all other fields in economics, is one in which complexity is used to disguise truth or to evade truth, not to reveal it. The process by which banks create money is so simple the mind is repelled. With something so important, a deeper mystery seems only decent." John Kenneth Galbraith (1908-), former professor of economics at Harvard, writing in 'Money: Whence it came, where it went' (1975).

As Nicolas Trist – secretary to President Andrew Jackson – said about the incredibly powerful privately owned Second Bank of the United States, "Independently of its misdeeds, the merepower, — the bare existence of such a power, — is a thing irreconcilable with the nature and spirit of our institutions." (Schlesinger, The Age of Jackson, p.102)

"Paper money eventually returns to its intrinsic value - - zero." –Voltaire

John Thore Stub Sneisen

The Economic Truth

Sign up for my newsletter and get free monthly economic updates, access to a free unpublished extra chapter, and a mini documentary on money and inflation by Josh Sigurdsson of World Alternative Media.

Follow me at:

http://www.theeconomictruth.org

And

Blog:

http://theworldeconomictruth.wordpress.com

Twitter: TrueEconomic

Facebook: The Economic Truth

References

From Wikipedia

Quote taken from Marco Polo's book the Travels of Marco Polo

Charts from The History of Fiat Paper Money by Ralph T. Foster

Source http://www.shadowstats.com page Charts from The History of Fiat Paper Money by Ralph T. Foster

Source http://www.thebubblebubble.com Source http://www.tradingeconomics.com Publicly available numbers

Source Kyle Bass

Source http://em.cbonds.com/countries/Venezuela-bond

Source Bank of International Settlements Quarterly Review 2015

Source Financial Data from

http://www.bloomberg.com

Source http://www.budget.gc.ca/2013/doc/plan/budget2013-eng.pdf

Source http://www.globalresearch.ca/world-health-organization-wont-back-down-from-study-linking-monsanto-to-cancer/5439840

Source http://articles.mercola.com/sites/articles/archive/2011/11/06/aspartame-most-dangerous-substance-added-to-food.aspx

Source Interactive Data via FactSet Research Systems

Source FirstWord Dossier

Source

http://www.sourcewatch.org/index.php/Correct

ions_Corporation_of_America

Source IMF Finance Department

Suggested Reading

I love reading and studying everything around me. On my webpage you will find documentaries and my research into 15+ economic systems. When you first jump into the rabbit hole of a non-governmental run education system you will never be able to come out again.

The last 10 years I have had the pleasure to be awakened to the universal laws that governs the world we live in. From my studies I bumped into the realm of Money, Economics and Geopolitics. These 3 topics caught my attention as I had many questions that were unanswered. I began a quest to understand to satisfy my curiosity, but was only met with new questions based on my new perception of the world.

You need to dedicate your life to learning. The most important topics are money and economics as they control your every move.

Here are the most important books I think you should read:

The History of Fiat Paper Money
By Ralph T. Foster

Rich Dad, Poor Dad
By Robert T. Kiyosaki

Planet Ponzi
By Mitch Feierstein

Investing in Gold and Silver

By Michael Maloney

The Creature From Jekyll Isle

By G. Edward Griffin

Currency Wars and The Death of Money

By James G. Rickards

Strategic Vision

By Zbigniew Brzezinski

Governing the World

By Mark Mazower

Think and Grow Rich

By Napoleon Hill

The End of the Free Market

By Ian Bremmer

The Devil's Derivatives

By Nicholas Dunbar

The Economics Book

By DK Publishing

The Law of Connection

By Michael J. Losier

The Law of Attraction

By Michael J. Losier

Coined

By Kabir Sehgal

Think Big

By Donald Trump and Bill Zanker

Leadership Gold

By John C. Maxwell

Outliers

By Malcom Gladwell

The Republic of Plato

By Allan Bloom

Rich Woman

By Kim Kiyosaki

Guide to Investing

By Robert T. Kiyosaki

Why We Want You to Be Rich

By Donald Trump and Robert T. Kiyosaki

Rich Dad's Conspiracy of The Rich

By Robert T. Kiyosaki

Retire Young Retire Rich

By Robert T. Kiyosaki

Rich Woman

By Kim Kiyosaki

The Secret

By Rhonda Byrne

7 Principles of Highly Effective People

By Stephen R. Covey

The Holy Bible

Jesus

By Deepak Chopra

Excuses Be Gone

By Wayne W. Dyer

The Four Agreements

By Don Miguel Ruiz

The Mastery of Love

By Don Miguel Ruiz

Awaken the Giant Within

By Anthony Robbins

Increase Your Financial IQ

By Robert T. Kiyosaki

www.ingramcontent.com/pod-product-compliance
Lightning Source LLC
Chambersburg PA
CBHW060551230426
43670CB00011B/1782